A SONG IN HIS HEART

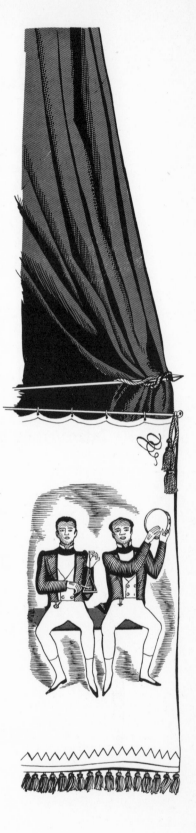

From the playbill collection at Keen's
English Chop House, New York City.

A SONG IN HIS HEART

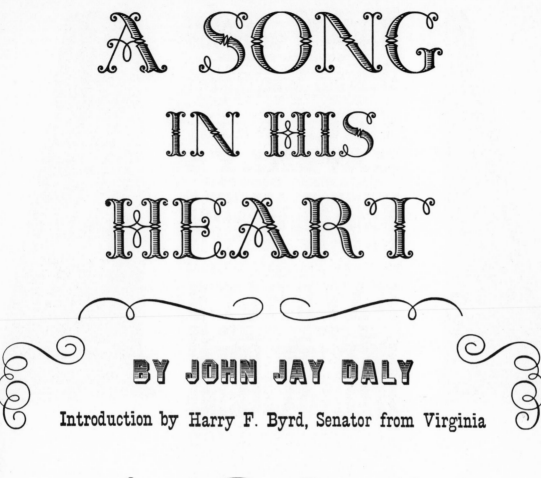

BY JOHN JAY DALY

Introduction by Harry F. Byrd, Senator from Virginia

Illustrated by Marian L. Larer

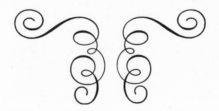

THE JOHN C. WINSTON COMPANY

Philadelphia · Toronto

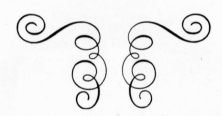

To the memory of James A. Bland
in recognition of his contribution
to American folk song

INTRODUCTION

ALTHOUGH THE PEOPLE OF VIRGINIA owe a debt of gratitude to James Bland for having given the Old Dominion State its official song, his countrymen in the other states are equally his benefactors.

During his lifetime, Bland composed over seven hundred songs, a number of which were outright contributions to Americana. Like Stephen Foster, with whom he has so often been compared, he felt the spiritual quality of the Negro race and succeeded in putting his feelings into words and music.

It is almost inconceivable that a man who had not been born and raised in Virginia could capture the nostalgic air that is evidenced in the lyrics and music of "Carry Me Back to Old Virginny." To have done so is a tribute to his genius just as much as it was to Foster's ability to compose "Swanee River," which many of his biographers claim he never saw.

The world in which Bland lived was a far different place than the one in which we live today. Born shortly before the War Between the States, he grew up in Washington during the reconstruction period.

He lived during a time that history will probably record as one of the most eventful periods in the annals of our country. The industrial age had become well advanced, the Victorian age was drawing to a close, and the twentieth century was about to begin. The nation was growing up, unaware of the tremendous part it was destined to play in world affairs.

The theater of which James Bland was so much a part reflected the times. The German band played in the beer gardens, the motion-picture industry had not yet been born and minstrelsy was the most popular form of theatrical entertainment. It was in this atmosphere that Bland, who instinctively loved an audience, excelled as a showman.

As we look back on the period in which Bland lived, it is hard not to feel a sense of envy for the serenity and security that the times offered. Europe seemed a long way off and Asia was indeed a remote and little-thought-of place. Our problems were purely American and everything else was foreign.

Life itself was simple, rich and full. Transportation moved at a leisurely pace. The isms that have since rocked the earth were unheard of and America thrived, prospered and grew. Times and conditions since then have changed greatly, but the principles on which this country were founded remain the same.

The story of James Bland is a testimonial to the greatness of America—a testimonial to the land in which an individual with ability and enterprise can make himself heard and his talents recognized.

We do not believe that Americans are better than other peoples, but they are much more fortunate. Let us keep this in mind and now, as we stand on the threshold of a new era—an era in which we look to America to lead a tired and weary world along paths of peace, may we pay tribute to a fellow American whose love of country gave us one of our best-loved state songs.

—HARRY F. BYRD
United States Senator from Virginia

CONTENTS

CHAPTER 1

JAMES BLAND THE MAN

A DILAPIDATED HEARSE, DRAWN BY two aged horses and followed by two carriages of mourners, started on its long trek through the streets of Philadelphia.

On that day in May, 1911, there was nothing unusual about the cortège to the casual observer. The automobile was still in its infancy and had not yet entirely supplanted the horse. Speed had not yet become a part of American life. Convention still demanded that the last journey of the deceased be conducted in a leisurely, dignified manner.

It had been but a few years since the horse car had given up the ghost to the street car, or "trolley" as it was commonly called in the city. The Market Street Subway was still a novelty, and the "pay-as-you-enter" was the latest innovation in city transportation. Philadelphians still rode the street cars on Sunday for recreation, and in the good old summertime they boarded the open trolleys that ran to Fairmount Park, where one could transfer to the Park trolley en route to Strawberry Mansion, a historic spot, or to Woodside Park for amusement.

The funeral procession, as it proceeded over the cobblestone streets, aroused no curiosity; for there was nothing pretentious about it; in fact, its shabbiness could only denote that it bore the remains of an impoverished citizen.

Turning onto the Spring Garden Street bridge, it crossed the Schuylkill River and turned onto the West River Drive. Even as the cortège passed over the dusty roads of suburban Bala-Cynwyd, farther on, it aroused little speculation. The local residents had long since become reconciled to the presence of the shabby, ill-kept cemetery that lay within their township. This particular cortège was no different from others that had preceded it to this spot.

What the people did not realize that day was that this burial ground was about to receive the mortal remains of one who was destined to become recognized as an outstanding member of the Negro race. Neither could they foresee that in later years the governor of a great Southern state would visit this hallowed ground to pay homage to a great American.

The late afternoon sun was slowly sinking as the procession pulled over the brow of the hill. Slowly it passed between the two stone pillars that marked the entrance to Merion Cemetery.

The interment of James A. Bland, composer of "Carry Me Back to Old Virginny" was about to take place—a man unhonored and forgotten by all but the handful of relatives and close friends in those two carriages. Although he was one of the greatest minstrels of his day and a composer whose music had swept over Europe and America, his grave was to remain unknown for over three decades.

* * * * *

James A. Bland was born during one of the most crucial, critical periods in the his-

tory of the United States. Compromise had broken down and the seeds of rebellion that were to result in the great struggle which nearly destroyed the nation had already been planted. During the year of Bland's birth, John Fremont's star was at its brightest. Two years later, with the resulting election of James Buchanan, Fremont's star had not only waned but had suffered a total eclipse. Gone, too, was the hope for preventing the disaster that was to rock the nation and send brother to fight against brother.

On October 22, 1854, young Bland first saw the light of day in Flushing, Long Island. Although his birth took place nine years before the Emancipation Proclamation, James Bland was born a free American, as the Blands had come from a long line of emancipated Negroes. The family was of Charleston, South Carolina, origin, but history leaves no record of how or why it was later transplanted to Long Island.

Young Jimmy, as he was to be known by his family and intimate friends, was one of a family of eight children and had the advantages of an educational background denied at that time to less fortunate members of his race. His father, Allen Bland, had attended a school in Charleston taught by Daniel Alexandrea Payne, who afterwards became a bishop in the African Methodist Church and also the founder of Wilberforce University. Later the father attended Oberlin College, in Ohio, where the registrar's report lists him as a student in the preparatory department from 1845 to 1848. The elder Bland had the distinction of being among the first college-trained Negroes, for he eventually graduated from Wilberforce University and later received his degree from the Law Department of Howard University. Apparently Allen Bland's quest for knowledge continued throughout the greater part of his life, for this postgraduate work was carried on at the same time his son James was also enrolled at Howard University.

James Bland's mother was also born of free parents in Wilmington, Delaware. One may readily realize that, although her education was limited to a greater degree than her husband's, nevertheless it is reasonable to suppose that she had the benefit of an elementary school education at least. It was under this environment that young Bland was raised. Whatever genius he might have had was no doubt due greatly to this influence.

Shortly after the War Between the States, Allen Bland moved his family to Washington, D. C., where he became an examiner in the United States Patent Office, the first Negro to be appointed to this office.

In Washington the Bland family occupied a dwelling in a row of houses built by General O. O. Howard, within a short distance of the Howard University campus. It was within the shadows of this institution that the story of James Bland really began. Young Bland attended the public schools of Washington, and later enrolled at Howard.

As we view the matter from present-day perspectives, it is hard to understand why Howard University failed to follow up the career of a former student who had won the fame that later was accorded James Bland. At the same time, we must remember that Howard, like most universities of its kind in that day, labored under a spell of missionary enthusiasm that amounted almost to religious fanaticism. Perhaps we can under-

stand the matter better when we read what Dr. Kelly Miller said in 1939. "Anything that smacked of vaudeville, comedians, and minstrels," this writer stated in the music magazine *Etude,* "was put under the ban; and the individual performers were held up as examples to be avoided. In those days students were not permitted to attend the legitimate theaters under penalty of dismissal, to say nothing of minstrel and vaudeville performances."

Unfortunately, today there is no clear-cut picture of James Bland's life other than the sparse facts discovered by various people who have been interested in perpetuating his memory. Dr. J. Francis Cooke, editor of *Etude,* in his desire to see Bland receive due recognition for his genius, has been largely instrumental in revealing much that had been forgotten. Dr. Cooke has long been interested in Bland's compositions and spent seven years searching for material on the great minstrel's life. He was particularly interested in finding Bland's grave, so that proper homage could be paid to the man who was recognized as one of the greatest troubadours of his day.

Dr. Cooke spent endless hours searching every reference on music known to the literary world. At rare intervals he ran across interesting bits of information. Once he wrote to Bland's publishers, the Oliver Ditson Co., of Boston, and received this answer: "I think Bland was a Negro." Later, from the Philadelphia Bureau of Vital Statistics, Dr. Cooke learned that the composer had died of tuberculosis at 1012 Wood Street, on May 5, 1911.

But still he could find no one who knew the location of the grave, nor could he unearth anything but the sparsest details of

Bland's life. It seemed as if the only data extant were confined within the musical manuscripts of the songs Bland wrote, and we are told that in his lifetime he wrote over seven hundred.

One day Dr. Cooke lectured at Howard University. Dr. Kelly Miller, who had written about Bland in 1939, and one of the foremost scholars of his race, was professor of mathematics, economics, and astronomy at the University. It was he who informed the music editor that Bland's grave lay about a mile from Dr. Cooke's own house in suburban Bala-Cynwyd!

By that time a considerable legend had grown up about the author of "Carry Me Back to Old Virginny." One writer, Dr. Miller told Dr. Cooke, had insisted that the composer was of Virginia slave parentage. Another stated that the ballad expressed the lament of a Virginia Negro slave who was sold in New Orleans in 1811. Many other stories about Bland were told to Dr. Cooke that day, some doubtless true; others undeniably fiction, but the most important thing Dr. Cooke wanted to know, and which he learned, was the location of Bland's grave.

He hurried back to Philadelphia and to Merion Cemetery. There was the grave, just as he had been told. When he spread the news, reporters rushed to his office, asking questions about the man whose name many of them had not even known before. At that time, and even today, many people believed that Stephen Foster wrote "Carry Me Back to Old Virginny," not realizing that Foster had died a number of years before the song was actually written.

The story also piqued the curiosity of one newspaper reporter in Philadelphia so much that he even stopped people on the street to ask them who had written "Oh, Dem Golden Slippers!" another of Bland's songs. He found only one person in ten who could answer correctly, and that despite the fact that for fifty years Philadelphia's famous Mummers had played this as the theme song of their annual New Year's Day parade.

In a word, ignorance about the man who had lived and died in Philadelphia, and who had given it what amounted to a musical symbol, was profound among the residents. And yet it is ironic that for a time Bland's name occupied an amount of newspaper space that would have pleased him even in his heyday. Editorials, feature stories, articles speculated on the great minstrel's life and works. The late Alexander Woollcott, noted wit and raconteur, even promised to "plug" a Bland memorial on his radio program, but died before he could carry through the plan.

James Bland's career took him to London several times. After nearly twenty years abroad, with occasional visits to his homeland, he returned to his favorite haunts in Washington. Despite his success abroad, he was apparently penniless, and one of his old friends gave him financial assistance.

By this time minstrels were on the wane and most people had forgotten the gay minstrel. His attempts to recapture his old flare were unsuccessful, for the musical that he wrote at this time was not a hit. Discouraged at his failure, he eventually wandered back to Philadelphia, the scene of his childhood. Unknown and forgotten, he died there of tuberculosis at the age of fifty-seven.

The discovery of Bland's grave, less than a decade ago, launched a campaign for proper recognition of this great composer of folk music. Bland himself probably never did more than visit "Old Virginny," but nevertheless the state of Virginia was touched. She felt that something should be done for the man who had written such a moving song bearing her name. The Lions Clubs of Virginia began to raise money for a memorial shaft to be placed on the Merion Cemetery grave in Bala-Cynwyd, Pa. As a preliminary tribute, Virginia adopted "Carry Me Back to Old Virginny" as the official state song. A problem of the correct spelling of the title temporarily delayed the adoption, however, but eventually the legislation was passed, with "Virginny" changed to a somewhat more decorous "Virginia."

At about the same time, W. C. Handy, called the "Daddy of the Blues," joined in services sponsored by the Philadelphia Council of the National Negro Congress in paying respects to Bland.

On July 15, 1946, the combined efforts of Dr. Cooke and the Lions Clubs of Virginia reached a climax. Governor William M. Tuck of Virginia, heading a delegation of Lions, attended ceremonies in Merion Cemetery and dedicated a monument at the Negro musician's grave. The Lions also provided sufficient money to permit a limited number of musical scholarships for Negro students in Virginia in memory of the composer.

"The history of people the world over is etched in the ballads they sing of their homes," said Governor Tuck to an audience, which included Mrs. Irene Jurix, of New York, one of the composer's two living sisters. "And their songs afford a glimpse into the character and mode of life of the singers. James Bland has put into ever-ringing verse and rime an expression of the feeling which all Virginians have for their state."

" 'Carry Me Back to Old Virginia' tells in inspiring song the innate patriotism and love of native heath of all our people, white and Negro alike. Let us all hope that peoples of all races may continue to sing this song and mean the message that it contains."

Ellis Loveless, assistant business manager of the Norfolk Newspapers, Inc., and Dr. Cooke, also addressed the gathering. John K. Donovan and Albert Large, district governors of the Lions, placed a wreath upon the new granite slab bearing the name "James A. Bland."

The homage may have been belated, but it was sincere. In a sense, Bland's country had made at least partial amends for thirty-five years of neglect.

CHAPTER 2

JIMMY BLAND THE BOY

AN AGED NEGRO, SEATED ON A TILTED, upturned peach basket, leaned against the high board fence and absorbed the bright September sunshine in lazy contentment. Holding an old banjo across his bony knees, he strummed the strings with his gnarled fingers as his right foot tapped in the dust of the alley with an easy, graceful rhythm. His rich, full voice accompanying the instrument penetrated the hush of the late afternoon. His plaintive melody conjured up visions of the Deep South and the joys and sorrows of the long-distant past with an occasional glimpse of hope for the future.

The patient stoicism so much a part of his race flowed from the strings of the banjo as water falling over a rock.

Suddenly from far down the street there came a rattling noise, accompanied by a young boy's voice. The noise grew in volume as the boy neared the old fellow sitting in the sun. The rattling and singing continued for a few seconds more. Then, abruptly, both stopped, and only the old man's voice and the tinkling of the banjo were heard.

Carried away by his own music, the banjoist closed his eyes and leaned farther back against the fence behind him. It was no effort to play and sing on a day like this, and his stiff hands plucked tirelessly at the strings. He would not stop playing merely because a small Negro boy clutching a stick was staring at him, with mouth open and his brown eyes wide with delighted amazement.

The boy, enthralled as he had never been before in his short life, squatted at the old man's feet. His eyes followed the player's fingers as they picked at the strings; as he watched, a lump formed in his throat.

Inspired by his listener, whom he continued to ignore, the old man played and sang for fifteen minutes. Then he stopped.

"Hello, boy," he said, trying to hide a look of pleasure. "Whar you come from?"

"Down the street."

"What yo' name?" asked the old man gruffly.

"Jimmy . . . Jimmy Bland." The boy took a deep breath. "Mister, that was first rate."

"What was fust rate?" inquired the old man, affecting not to understand.

"That stuff you were playin'. Mister, what's that thing called?"

"This?" The old man held up the banjo. "This here, boy, is a banjo."

"A banjo!" Jimmy sucked his under lip between his white teeth. "Mister," he said after a slight pause, "how much does a banjo cost?"

"Sho! I wouldn't know, cause I've had this here musical instrument close onto twenty-five years. And at that, it was give to me." He closed his eyes, his forehead deeply wrinkled in concentration. "Might cost mebbe two, mebbe five, mebbe more dollars," he replied at length.

Jimmy's face fell and his mouth quivered.

"That's a lot of money, mister!" he exclaimed.

"Lot of money!" cried the old man. "Lot of money for a fine musical instrument like this here? That ain't much money, boy."

"For *me* it is. Mister, is it hard to learn to play a banjo?"

"Some folks pick it up right easy. Others never do learn. I picked it up tolably quick."

Jimmy Bland nodded and continued to gaze at the little round box from which magic had flowed only a few moments before.

"Mister," he said in a small voice, "would . . . would you play and sing some more for me?"

"I just got done playin' and singin', boy! I'm all played out now. Just want to sit in the sun and rest myself."

"I wish you'd play just one more tune! I want to see how you move your fingers over those strings. You play so nice and sing so sweet."

The flattery was too much for the old man. "Well, just one more." He took up the banjo, crossed one leg over the other, and began to play another of his nameless spirituals, his foot again beating time in the dust.

Jimmy could scarcely contain his joy. He opened his mouth as if to join in the singing, but quickly closed it for fear of annoying the old man.

It was a tender song that the old Negro played—a song of evening after work in the cotton fields was done, and of tired bodies relaxing as the sun sank behind a clump of sycamore trees in the distance. It told of the anguish of slavery, and pathetically voiced the hope that an after life would mean the end of all sorrow.

The last notes died away and the old man laid aside the banjo. He got up, shook himself and began to shuffle off, little puffs of dust rising as his big feet plodded along.

Sensing that he was now dismissed, the little boy trotted off in another direction—toward the tailor shop where Jimmy's father worked, and where his brothers and sisters children lived and played together.

As Jimmy walked along the Philadelphia street that autumn afternoon in 1867, he knew that never in his life had he wanted anything so much as he wanted a banjo. At Christmastime he had seen many fascinating toys displayed in the shop windows, but had long since learned to accept the hard fact that his father could not think of buying such expensive things. Once or twice Jimmy had cried softly to himself in the bed where he slept with one of his brothers. But the next day the yearning usually disappeared, and he was happy with the playthings he already had.

But this was different. He knew that the longing for a banjo would always be with him. Somehow he must get one.

"Mebbe two dollars, mebbe five dollars, mebbe more," the old man had said. How in the world could a twelve-year-old boy get that much money? His father had enough trouble finding money to feed and clothe his brood, and sometimes life was not easy in the Bland household.

He would ask his father about the banjo anyhow. His Pa could do anything he wanted to do; he might think of some way for Jimmy to earn the money. A spark of hope filled his heart as he turned the corner of the cobblestoned street where the tailor shop was. His father was a bright man, Jimmy thought proudly. He might be only a tailor, but people respected him because he seemed to know so much. Smart men

who brought their clothes to the shop often lingered so they could talk with Allen Bland for a spell.

Jimmy was so engrossed in his thoughts that he was almost run over by a beer truck drawn by four glossy horses. The red-faced driver jerked the animals in violently and glared at the little boy.

"You'd make a right cute little angel," he cried, "gettin' yourself fitted for golden slippers, boy?"

Jimmy smiled apologetically. Even as the cumbersome dray rumbled down the street, the music was singing in his blood again.

"Golden slippers," the little boy murmered to himself. "Golden slippers," he sang softly as he walked on. What a pretty idea that was! Of course, angels wear golden slippers along with their wings and halos! The music still rang in his ears as he halted a few yards from the shop. Golden slippers and golden music glided out of his mind and a wave of depression engulfed him, as he saw his father sitting on a stool, his head bent over a piece of cloth, stitching, stitching, as he did every day, from early morning until late at night. Jimmy couldn't explain that wave of sadness, or why the sight of his father caused it.

A banjo? Jimmy might as well ask his father for a carriage and horses like those rich people on Walnut and Spruce Streets drove in on their way to church on Sundays!

As Jimmy entered the shop, his father looked at him over his spectacles. In some ways the little fellow was his favorite, although he frequently had doubts about his son's future. Jimmy seemed to have a deep aversion to study, but his father never felt entirely right about bearing down too hard on him. There was something about Jimmy

OH, DEM GOLDEN SLIPPERS!

that the father could not understand, but which he nevertheless respected. In a way, he seemed to sense that this boy of his was different and could not be judged by ordinary standards.

"Hello, Jimmy," he said. "Where have you been?"

Suddenly Jimmy was overcome with embarrassment. He didn't want to tell his father about the banjo and what it had meant to him.

"Oh, just down the street," he replied indifferently. "Walking around and looking at things."

"You seem to be excited about something, son. Kind of like you'd seen something special."

"Oh, no!" Jimmy replied. "Nothing much. Saw an old man playing a banjo, Pa. It was pretty."

"A banjo does make nice music. Now, son, take this suit around to Mr. Baker, will you? He's been waiting for it."

"Sure, Pa."

Jimmy folded the suit over his skinny arm and turned to the door.

"Pa, how much does a banjo cost?"

"Haven't the least idea. Why?"

"Oh, I was just wondering. Just thought it sounded so nice."

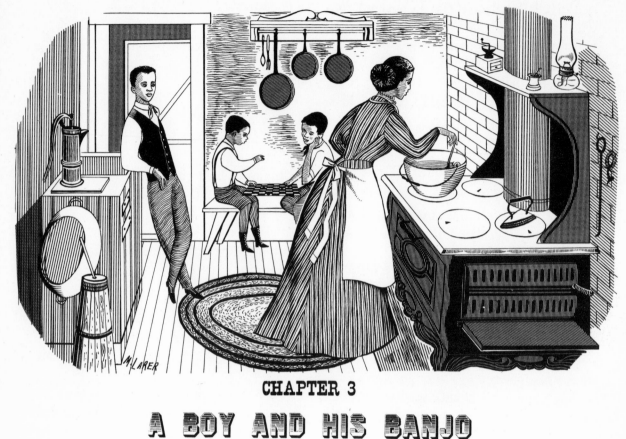

CHAPTER 3

A BOY AND HIS BANJO

ROM THE DAY JIMMY BLAND FIRST heard the old Negro play the banjo, his desire to own one became almost an obsession. His main impulse was to conceal the feeling that had swept over him that autumn day. The more he thought about it, the more reluctant he was to speak of his longing for a banjo. But the music it had made echoed over and over in his young ears.

His afternoons were devoted to delivering clothes for his father, and Jimmy had scruples about faithfully carrying out this job. Still, somehow, when he had finished his deliveries, he always found himself loitering in the vicinity of the alley. As he stood there with his narrow back against the board fence, it seemed that the music was ever present, waiting for his listening ear.

A week after his meeting with the old banjo player, Jimmy summoned up his courage enough to enter a pawnshop to ask the price of a banjo that he had seen hanging in the window, at which he had gazed so longingly. The proprietor was waiting on a customer as Jimmy approached the counter, and the boy was tempted to turn and flee. At that moment, the customer finished his business and Jimmy had no choice but to remain.

"What'll you have?" asked the old man, who wore a black alpaca coat and glasses. "Any diamond rings to pawn?"

"No, sir," Jimmy gasped, in a state of total irresolution.

"Come on, boy. Speak up. What'll you have?"

"I was wondering . . . about that banjo you got in the window."

"Wondering? What about?"

"How much does it cost?" Jimmy managed to ask.

"That's a fine instrument, boy. We've got it up for ten dollars." He glanced at Jimmy kindly. "Don't look like it's your kind of money, though. Might shave it to eight dollars," he added, when he saw the disappointment in the boy's face.

Jimmy turned away. "Just shopping around," he said lamely. "Just want to see what I can get before I buy anything," repeating phrases his mother used so often in the market.

Overcome with shyness, he almost ran to the door. With his hand on the knob, he paused and turned toward the pawnbroker.

"Mister," he stammered, "would . . . would . . ."

The man waited for the sentence to be completed. When it wasn't, he said, "Would what?"

"Mister, would . . ." cried Jimmy in a burst of self-confidence, "could I just *hold* the banjo a minute? I won't hurt it any."

"Well, maybe. I guess you can't hurt it. But take care you don't drop it."

The pawnbroker went to the window, and returning, placed the instrument in Jimmy's hands. The boy's eyes filled with tears, and he held the banjo as if it were a piece of fine china or crystal. He folded it to his scrawny chest, letting his hands caress the strings. If only he could sweep his fingers over the strings the way the old man had done! He closed his eyes, and knew that he too could make that music.

The pawnbroker's voice aroused him.

"Well, boy, maybe some day you'll get that money. Those things don't move so fast. If you come back six months from now with the eight dollars, chances are we'll still have it here waiting for you. You go and find the money."

It was hopeless, Jimmy thought as he walked down the street. Eight dollars was as impossible to attain as the sun, the moon, or the stars. Even if he could figure out a way to make the money, he knew what it would be when he had it in his hands. He would be sure to think of all the things that eight dollars could buy for his brothers and sisters.

Then a thought struck him. Suppose he were to *make* a banjo? Jimmy had studied the one in the hands of the old man in the alley and the grand instrument in the pawnshop. Of course, he couldn't hope to equal the final product. But maybe . . . just maybe . . . he could figure out something that he could at least play a little bit. He'd make believe the real music!

It was his secret during the odd moments that he spent in the cellar under the tailor shop with his father's rusty saw and the wires he managed to find behind some lumber.

First, out of those pieces of lumber he sawed out curved pieces for the top and bottom of the banjo. The sides presented a problem because he had no idea how to bend wood. But he realized that if he could bend the sides to take the shape of the curved top and bottom pieces, he could then glue them together.

One of the workmen in a near-by lumber yard told him that steam would bend wood into desired shapes, so one day while his mother was at the market he heated a kettle of water and bent the side pieces into the necessary curves. From a cabinet maker he obtained enough glue to complete his home-made banjo.

One afternoon after he finished his chores, Jimmy sneaked the instrument out of the house. He was ashamed of it; he would have been horrified if any member of the family had seen it. But to him it was beautiful because it resembled the ones that he had seen in the hands of the old banjoist and in the pawnshop window.

Impelled by a dim superstition, Jimmy went directly to the alley with his little homemade banjo. Perhaps the sun-blistered boards of the fence had made some contribution to the total effect that had moved him so deeply, or it could have been the ankle-deep dust of the alley itself. He felt that if he too were to sit on an upturned fruit basket and tap his bare toes in the dust as the old man had done, he would be inspired.

The alley was empty when Jimmy arrived to test out his sad little music maker. The sun was bright, and it warmed his body like a blessing. He began to play. The sounds made by the jerry-built instrument were as utterly discordant as possible, but he did not really hear them. As he strummed inharmoniously, the little boy sang in his shrill voice. He didn't know what he was singing, but to him the satisfaction was nearly complete. He was making movements that produced sound, and he was singing in ac-

companiment to the sound, just as the old man had done.

He closed his eyes, the better to evoke the music that he wanted to hear, and also for better imitation of the old man. He was alone in the alley, and with all his mind and heart he concentrated, intent on creating once more the wonderful sensation he had experienced when he heard the old man.

Jimmy did not hear the footsteps that approached. When he opened his eyes, he stopped playing immediately, for before him stood a tall, strongly built boy who gazed at him with insolent eyes and sneering mouth. Jimmy dropped the banjo to his side as if to hide its imperfections. The two regarded each other silently.

"What's all that noise you been makin'?"

Jimmy clutched the banjo more tightly. He made no reply. Sensing danger to his beloved instrument, he grasped it in both hands, hugging it to his chest.

"What's it s'posed to be?" the other boy inquired, stretching out his hand.

"N-nothing."

"Must be s'posed to be somethin'. What's it s'posed to be?"

"A . . . a banjo."

"Lemme see it," the big boy demanded.

Jimmy moved a step sidewise. He knew the other boy now; his name was Willie Carter, but in the neighborhood he was nicknamed "Bully," because he loved to pick fights with smaller boys. Jimmy's first instinct was to get away as fast as he could, to save his banjo. He was quick on his feet; he felt sure he could escape. But he couldn't bear the ignominy of running away.

Willie Carter stepped forward.

"Lemme see it!" he demanded brutally, grasping at the banjo again. "I just want to see what's been makin' all that noise." His sinewy fingers wrapped themselves around the lathe that served as the finger board. He tugged at it. Jimmy tugged in return.

Terrified by the thought that in the tug of war the precious banjo might be broken, Jimmy finally surrendered it. He stood with his arms at his sides, nervously clenching and unclenching his fists while Willie Carter subjected the instrument to a contemptuous inspection. Finally Willie tucked the banjo under his arm and strummed a few notes, at the same time burlesquing Jimmy's singing, rolling his eyes as he sang.

"Now give it back to me," Jimmy begged. "Please give it back. It's . . . it's mine."

"Want to look at it some more. Where'd you git it, boy?"

"I made it myself."

"Naw! Thought it musta cost a lotta money at some swell shop by the looks of it."

Jimmy reached for the banjo, tears of rage welling in his eyes. Willie Carter deftly jerked it away, and ignoring Jimmy, continued to toy with the banjo.

"How long'd it take you to make this here thing?"

"None of your business!" Jimmy shouted suddenly. "Give it back to me or I'll . . ."

That seemed to be what Willie Carter had been waiting for. He whirled and crouched.

"You'll what?" he asked. "You'll what, boy? Go on and say it. I like to hear kids like you tell me what they think they'll do."

Jimmy's fists were so tightly clenched that his fingernails dug into his palms, but he was so desperately afraid that he scarcely dared move.

Suddenly Willie Carter laughed, and as he laughed, he dropped the banjo to the ground, deliberately raised a foot and drove it through the sound box.

Jimmy leaped forward, his fists hammering out like bony little pistons. He was sobbing with fury as he fought, the tears running down his cheeks. Once or twice he knew the satisfaction of his flesh crushing against the flesh of the monster, but it was not for long.

Willie Carter prided himself on his prowess as a fighter; he dreamed of the day when he would be a professional. He crouched and bobbed his head, his arms adroitly crooked. The exultant grin remained on his face and when Jimmy's fists landed, Willie Carter merely laughed, throwing his head back. He was toying with Jimmy, reveling in the knowledge of his superior strength and agility.

As Jimmy continued to flail, Willie Carter suddenly leaped back a step or two. He dropped his arms to his side, but continued to weave and bob expertly as Jimmy ineffectually struck at his face.

"Maybe you need fightin' lessons just like you need music teachin'," he said. "Maybe I'll give you the first lesson right now."

Jimmy didn't see the fist that connected with his jaw, and he didn't feel the ground as his back struck it and he rolled over. He was aware of nothing whatever except a tremendous darkness. As he lay in the dust of the alley, a trickle of blood ran from his nose, mingling with the tears that still gleamed wet on his cheeks.

Willie Carter stared at his prostrate victim for a moment. Then, lithely, he bent over and inspected Jimmy's face. Satisfied that the boy would regain consciousness in a few minutes, he clapped his hat cockily on his head and strutted down the alley.

[15]

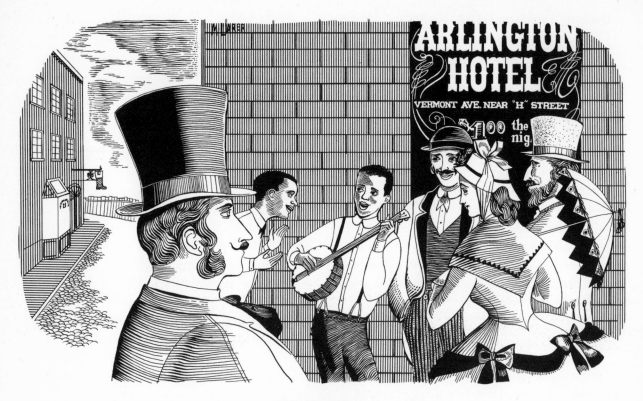

CHAPTER 4

A SILVER LINING

THE RESOUNDING SILENCE IN THE alley was penetrated by street noises—the rattle of a cab; the voices of two women talking over a back fence; the cries of a fish vendor peddling his wares.

Jimmy rolled over on his back and opened his eyes. His jaw was swollen and it throbbed unmercifully, but he was scarcely conscious of the pain as rage and grief rose within him. He remembered now what had happened, and for a while he avoided looking at the banjo.

Perhaps it had all been a dream. Perhaps his precious instrument had not been de-stroyed after all. Flinging out an arm, he scratched his hand against one of the broken pieces of the box. His fingers closed on the wood as he picked up the broken banjo. At that moment he knew that if he had the strength, he could pummel the life out of Willie Carter.

Holding the shattered sound box on his knees, Jimmy Bland sat up. The banjo was gone, wrecked beyond repair. As he gazed at it, a ray of encouragement crept into his heart. It was gone, but *he* had made it, and if he could make one instrument, he could make another! Perhaps the second one would be better than the first. With that thought, the anger he had felt toward Willie Carter was forgotten.

"That's it," he muttered as he stood up, his large, melancholy eyes glowing. "I'll just make me another. That's the way I can beat that old Willie Carter."

As he neared home, Jimmy grew increasingly conscious of the pain and the swelling of his jaw. Despite the assurance that he had just given himself, he was ashamed of the licking he had received.

What he wanted to do was sneak down to the cellar, hide the broken banjo, and start to think about the one to replace it. But Jimmy forgot that it was growing dark, and that his parents might be concerned about him. At the door to the shop he met his mother.

"Jimmy," she said gently, but gravely, "we were worried about you. Why are you so late?" Her quick eyes noticed the broken banjo in her son's thin arms. Jimmy stalled. "Oh, I got talking to a fellow down the street, and first thing I knew it was dark."

His mother continued to look at him, and her steady gaze made him more ashamed of lying than of admitting what had happened. The grief over the loss of his banjo welled up in him again, and he forgot his attempt at nonchalance.

The shop was illuminated only by the flickering light of an oil lamp in the back room, and there Jimmy told his mother the whole story, including his experience with the old man in the alley.

Without making a comment, his mother took him by the hand and led him to the stove where a kettle was steaming. She poured hot water on a cloth and made him lie down while she patiently applied the hot cloth to his swollen jaw.

"Is Pa home?" Jimmy asked her. "He'll likely be mad at me, won't he, Ma?"

"He's not home just now," his mother said, "but he won't be mad at you, Jimmy." She paused and looked at her son. "Your Pa will feel about it just the way I do."

"But, Ma, I should have been able to lick that Willie Carter. I should have been able to take the banjo away from him and beat him up."

"That doesn't matter, Jimmy. That wouldn't have been so important. What was important was the fact that you didn't run away."

After he had his supper, Jimmy went up to the room where all the children slept on cots ranged in rows like a dormitory. Jimmy shared a cot with his brother Ivanhoe. It was a cheap canvas affair, but Mrs. Bland had managed to make it comfortable with cotton wadding and an old quilt.

Alfie and all the others were asleep when Jimmy crept between the covers. For some reason he was extremely happy. He felt that his mother thought he had done something very fine, although he didn't know just what it was. He couldn't see why not running away from a fight should be so remarkable.

In spite of his mother's treatment, his jaw still ached enough to keep him awake, and he heard his father come into the house. Jimmy knew what would happen now, because the same thing often happened on other nights when Jimmy didn't fall asleep immediately. His mother and father sat together in the combination sitting and dining room for a long time. Sometimes Jimmy's father read aloud and often Jimmy crept to the door so that he could listen. Sometimes his father read the Bible; sometimes it was

Shakespeare, or interesting stories from the newspaper.

Alfie was sleeping heavily, so Jimmy slipped off the cot and crept over to the door. Tonight, however, he did not hear his father reading. Instead, there was a steady hum of conversation. Jimmy occasionally heard his own name mentioned as he stood with his ear pressed against the drafty crack in the doorway.

"Allen, I almost cried when he came in with that banjo all smashed," he heard his mother say.

His father mumbled something Jimmy could not hear.

"He made it all himself, and then that little monster broke it. I wish we could punish him for that. He nearly broke Jimmy's heart along with the banjo."

Jimmy then heard his father talking about a job. He wasn't quite sure what his father meant by "job," and he was wondering about it when he heard his mother say:

"If you get that job, we'll try to get him a real one. A boy with that much courage deserves it."

"Don't know whether I'll get it . . . Wish I did," his father said. "No mail today. It'd mean so much if I'd get it! But the war hasn't been over very long and the people still feel the same way about colored folk."

"Allen," said Jimmy's mother, "I just have a feeling that you'll get it. I had the same feeling when I knew our boy had made that banjo all by himself."

Jimmy's father laughed as he promised, "If I get that job, Mama, he'll get his banjo, all right."

Jimmy tiptoed back to the cot, but before he slid between the covers, he kneeled at the side. He prayed for his father to get the job

—whatever it was. He prayed that the job would bring him a real banjo. If it did, then getting licked wouldn't matter.

In the days that followed, Jimmy sensed a tension in the house. The other children seemed to be unaware of it, so he did not speak of it to them, but sometimes he would find his father sitting on his stool in the tailor shop, needle poised over a piece of suiting, staring into space.

The tension was evident in the subdued excitement with which his mother greeted the infrequent visits of the mailman. Allen Bland had never been one to show great interest in receiving letters, but now Jimmy noticed that his father was invariably at the door waiting for the familiar uniform to appear. When the mailman dropped off a letter or card, Jimmy's mother appeared immediately, out of nowhere, it seemed, to watch Allen Bland's face eagerly. And each time the mailman came, or when he passed by without leaving any letters, Jimmy observed sadness on his parents' faces.

Once he heard his father say, as he returned to his work:

"It just isn't in the cards. They'll never give it to me."

"But I know they will," his mother replied. "We'll just have to be patient."

It was a day or two after this conversation that Jimmy wandered into the kitchen, shortly before supper. A pot of stew was simmering on the stove and his mother sat near by, the tears running down her cheeks. She wept silently, and Jimmy's heart turned over at the sight as he stood unobserved in the doorway.

Something very dreadful must have happened to make his mother cry, because he had never seen her cry before. Timidly he approached her.

"Ma," he said, as he touched her, "don't cry. Please don't cry."

"It's nothing, Jimmy," she smiled through her tears at him, "I'm just being silly."

"What's the matter, Ma? Can't you tell me? I'm twelve years old now. I'm old enough to know about things."

"Perhaps you're right, Jimmy. I will tell you. Your father's been trying to get a job in Washington. You wouldn't understand what it was if I told you, but it would mean a lot to him and to all of us. He could go to school at night and study law the way he wants to. And we'd live much better."

"Ma," he said, "I guess you've prayed plenty for Pa to get the job, haven't you?"

"I certainly have, Jimmy. All the time, and I feel sure the Lord won't let us down. I was just crying because it seems to be taking so long."

"I'll pray too, Ma. I'll pray all the time, too. Maybe that'll help."

"I'm sure it will, Jimmy."

The very next day the mailman brought a long, official-looking envelope. Jimmy was on an errand when it arrived, but he knew that the tidings were good when he saw his parents' faces as he entered the tailor shop.

Allen Bland was still holding the letter. His hands were trembling, but his face shone with joy. Jimmy's mother stood beside him, reading the letter over his shoulder for the tenth time at least.

"Jimmy!" she cried. "Your father got the job and we're going to Washington next week!"

Allen Bland turned to his son. "Jimmy, your mother told me about the fight you had." He smiled. "Let's walk over to the pawnshop and see what we can do about that banjo!"

CHAPTER 5

THE BOY TROUBADOUR

HEN JIMMY'S FATHER moved his family to Washington, the nation was young — reborn after the blood purge of the War Between the States. The United States had just purchased Alaska from Russia for the modest sum of $7,000,000, plus a fee of $200,000 to the Russian-American Trading Company. The House of Representatives had instigated the impeachment of President Andrew Johnson, but his removal from office had been prevented by the vote of one Senator, who rose from a sickbed to cast a not-guilty ballot.

Ulysses S. Grant, with Schuyler Colfax,

Speaker of the House, running for vice president, was elected on the Republican ticket, and followed Johnson in the White House. The country went on an untrammeled postwar spending spree, which, among other things, resulted in the construction of the Union Pacific Railroad, the Credit Mobilier Scandal, and the corner on gold engineered by Jay Gould and Jim Fisk.

Money and the power that it represented were the deities of the time, and it was considered smart to be tricky. The robber barons were in full power, and, partaking of a species of latter-day feudalism, the nation's philosophy appeared to be that rich people were necessarily the finest citizens, no matter what evil they wrought. Labor unions, a struggling nonentity, were considered conceptions of the Devil himself.

"The trade union, originated under the European system, destroys liberty," thundered Henry Ward Beecher, the outstanding preacher in the country. Beecher solemnly stated that "the man who cannot live on bread and water is not fit to live."

Apparently Beecher expressed the feeling of a vast majority. When brakemen on the Erie Railroad went on strike for higher wages, Gould and Fisk not only refused to talk with the strikers but dispatched a gang of New York ruffians to break up the "revolt" by the simple expedient of beating the strikers. The newspapers hailed this achievement as a fine example of public spirit, and they were supported in their editorial by a flood of letters to the editor trumpeting variations of the same theme.

Although it was the nation's capital, the Washington of the 1860's and 1870's was a long way behind the city it is today. It was merely a sprawling good-time town, filled with gamblers, carpetbaggers, and real-estate agents peddling such developments as Pipe Town and Cow Town. It boasted only one paved street, Pennsylvania Avenue.

Two principal railroads channeled into the city: the Baltimore and Ohio, and the Baltimore and Potomac, whose depot, at the corner of B and 6th Streets, was to be the scene of President James A. Garfield's assassination. Indicative of the city's large transient population were the number of hotels. Among the best-known was Willard's, better known as "Old Lady Willard's Boarding House." It was located across the street from Newspaper Row, on Pennsyl-

vania at the corner of 14th Street. Other famous hotels of the day were the Arlington, on Vermont Avenue near H Street, and Ebbitt's on I Street. Rates on the American Plan ranged from four dollars to five dollars per week. Lodgings on the European Plan could be had for one dollar per night for a single room. Two persons could have a double room with parlor attached for two dollars each.

The five-cent fare prevailed on the city's rather extensive horse-car omnibus lines, which included the Washington and Georgetown Street Railway, incorporated in 1862, the Columbia Line and the Metropolitan Line. The latter charged seven cents for single rides, but passengers could buy ten rides for fifty cents.

Cab service was abundant and comparatively cheap. A one-horse carriage was available for one or two riders at about seventy-five cents an hour between five A.M. and shortly after midnight. Rates during the "wee" hours from twelve-thirty to five A.M. jumped to the rather odd figure of one dollar and twelve cents.

For the entertainment and edification of the city's approximately 110,000 inhabitants, there were two principal theaters: Ford's, on 9th Street south of Pennsylvania Avenue, where Abraham Lincoln was assassinated, and the National, on E Street between 13th and 14th. On their stages, stock companies offered standard comedies and tragedies during the winter months, varied by Italian, German, and English operas. In warm weather, Washingtonians amused themselves and their guests by taking a ferry at the 7th Street Wharf down the Potomac to Mount Vernon. The ferry chugged out of Washington at 10 A.M.

every day except Sunday, leaving Mount Vernon for the return trip at 4 P.M. The dollar and a half fare did not include admission to the historic home of George Washington or to the grounds.

This was the Washington of Bland's day, and for a short time after they arrived there the family lived at 15th and L Streets, a few blocks from the White House. Later they moved to Howard Row, opposite the newly founded Howard University, where Allen Bland took a law course in the evenings.

First thought of as a theological school, Howard University came into being at a prayer meeting in November, 1866. Actually, it opened as a normal school in 1867 in an abandoned dance hall and saloon, which served as a combination dormitory and dissecting room. In the beginning, few Negroes were sufficiently educated for entrance requirements. Most of the early applications came from poor white young men and girls, but gradually Negroes applied and were admitted, for General Howard was utterly devoid of racial prejudice.

For all its racial tolerance, the rules of the university were very strict, and military influence was much in evidence. Students were roused at dawn; they dressed in uniform, responded to roll calls and drilled. They were required to salute members of the faculty and to stand at attention in the presence of trustees. It is not to be wondered at that the authorities at Howard disapproved of minstrels, vaudeville, and anything to do with the theater. However, the strength of the youthful composer's urge was too great, and his country can be thankful for that powerful obstinacy of his. He stuck to music and forsook his studies. His father may have despaired and Jimmy may

have sorrowed, but if Jimmy had not persisted there might never have been such songs as "Carry Me Back to Old Virginny" and "In the Evening by the Moonlight."

Incorporated by General O. O. Howard for the education of youth without reference to sex or color, Howard University eventually became a Negro institution. The school comprised three principal buildings: the university building, four stories high, containing the philosophical, lecture and recitation rooms, library, museum and offices; Miner Hall, which was the women's dormitory, with the professors' residences at each end; and the Normal Building, used for classes and chapel services.

Young Jimmy went to a new school for Negroes, but the banjo his father had bought him and the music he could make with it tended to wean Jimmy from the path Allen Bland wanted his children to follow. Fiercely ambitious to accomplish things his race had never before attempted, Allen Bland had not patience with anything resembling laziness, and in his opinion, Jimmy's incessant banjo-playing was superficial. He wanted his son to be a scholar. But where the elder Bland failed to win any great distinction for all his efforts, the son later achieved fame and considerable wealth through the medium his father had held in such contempt. It was as natural for Jimmy to make music as it was for a bird to sing. The banjo that Allen Bland had given his son was as much a part of Jimmy as his right arm, and he rapidly became its master.

At the time the family moved to Washington, Jimmy Bland was a tall thin boy of about twelve, inclined to be more quiet and serious than the average boy of his age. His features were regular, his hair wavy

DANCING ON DE KITCHEN FLOOR

black, and his complexion medium-light. In the early evening hours young Bland and his many friends, both Negro and white, would stroll through the streets and sing popular songs of the day. The melodies that flowed from the strings of Jimmy's banjo made him a great favorite with any group. Very often the songs that they played and sang were the compositions of Stephen Foster, and it is highly probable that Foster's style influenced James Bland greatly. Years later he admitted to a friend that he admired Stephen Foster's work more than that of any other composer.

Not long after the Blands moved to Washington, Jimmy fell into the habit of wandering about the city, playing and singing for whatever pennies the passers-by would toss in his direction. He loved his music, but at the same time he almost hated it, because of the conflict it caused between him and his father. Life without music and the happiness it gave would have been a prison to Jimmy Bland. Often after the rest of the household was asleep, the youthful troubadour would creep out, sometimes climbing down a drain pipe, his banjo strapped across his back, to walk the streets, making music merely for his own entertainment.

Nearly every afternoon Jimmy and his banjo visited Lafayette Square, across the street from the Executive Mansion. This was a rendezvous for the boys and girls of the neighborhood. It wasn't long before the young musician caught the attention of the well-dressed people who strolled through the park to near-by dining clubs and restaurants. Up to that time Jimmy had never played professionally, although he did rely on the coins that his wealthy listeners tossed

to him for his pocket money and even at that time he was enough of a showman to glory in an audience.

Late one afternoon, just as Jimmy was about to go home for supper, he noticed a distinguished-looking man with an erect military bearing standing near Clark Mills's equestrian statue of Andrew Jackson. The one-man audience stood with his head cocked to one side, a dreamy expression in his eyes. The reaction in Jimmy was immediate. He played as he hadn't played all afternoon, because he had a feeling that the man was destined to mean something to his own future.

But Jimmy pretended not to notice the man beside the statue. He reached the end of his song, tucked the banjo under his arm, and sauntered away.

"Come here, boy," called the stranger.

Jimmy walked toward him leisurely. "Yes, sir," he said.

"That's mighty nice music you make."

"Glad you like it, sir."

"How'd you like to play in a hotel?"

"Oh . . . oh, man!" Jimmy stammered. "Would I like it!"

"Well, I want to introduce you to a friend of mine who's on the lookout for fellows like you. My name is Allen—General James Allen. What's yours?"

Haltingly Jimmy told him. Then the two started off, the stranger leading the way. The result of that chance meeting was an introduction to John Chamberlin, one of the leading hotel men of Washington, who was always eagerly searching for musical talent and unusual entertainment to appeal to his guests. At the time Chamberlin's was a gathering place for the élite of the city. As soon as he had heard the fourteen-year-old boy perform, Chamberlin recognized the boy's drawing power. He immediately hired young Jimmy for afternoon and evening performances as well as for private parties and helped the young troubadour work out a routine. James Bland, once playing in the streets for pennies, now found himself a professional performer.

At first Jimmy's parents offered objections, but the family's need for extra money was great. Here was an opportunity that could not be passed by. By nature, Jimmy was a night owl. Many times, after performing at Chamberlin's and after his parents thought him safely in bed, he sneaked out of the house and appeared on programs in the city's hotels and summer gardens. These youthful experiences may have done little to improve his health, but the training gave him a confidence that he was never to lose.

At first he played and sang only the recognized song hits of the era. Later, when he was about fifteen, he began to contribute short compositions of his own—compositions that he had not yet learned to transfer to paper. Unconsciously, he was acquiring his trade by constant practice. While other boys played, young Bland plucked at his banjo, his long, slender fingers moving over the strings so rapidly that they seemed to fly. In addition, he could do tricks with the instrument, spin it around his head without breaking the rhythm of his music; play it behind his back or under his knees. He also knew how to tone down the tin-panny sound of the instrument of that period by padding the under surface with raw cotton. He was dominated by a driving passion—a passion that would not let him rest; a passion to make music of his own, music that people would know had been composed by James

A. Bland, and no other. The banjo and Bland were blended, one with the other, as General Allen expressed it in later years as he recalled the music of the "Negro Stephen Foster."

He had never been a robust boy, and in his teens he was rather delicate. There was hardly any weight to him—a gangling youngster who seemed all legs and arms. When at last he did reach his full growth, he never at any time weighed more than one hundred and fifty pounds. According to those who said they remembered him from his Washington days, he stood about five feet ten inches.

"Jimmy Bland was a nice-looking kid, happy-go-lucky, affable, good-natured," according to General Allen, who had started Jimmy off professionally. When the general retired from the Army, he made his home at the Army-Navy Club in Washington, where he was served his last Canvasback dinner, in memory of his membership in the old Canvasback Club. Lomack, the original waiter of the club, served him. Lomack had worked at Harvey's and Chamberlin's and had known Jimmy Bland when Jimmy was in his prime.

"That Bland boy was out of this world," Lomack once said. "I remember him well. I remember when he played at Harvey's and when he played at Chamberlin's. He was a popular entertainer around Washington from the time he was fourteen until he went away, in his middle twenties, to join the minstrel shows. Even then he didn't stay away long. Whenever a show closed, Bland came back to visit his father and mother. He liked Washington better than any other city."

The waiter also recalled that Bland had

a quartet that harmonized with him as he sang and played the banjo. The four good singers he had picked up rehearsed regularly, so when he got a job he could appear as a soloist or else in the company of his quartet. And he got top prices.

"They didn't fool Jimmy Bland very much," Lomack continued, and smiled. "He always got good money for his act, much more than the waiters did. And many of us wished we could play like he could. But he was in a class by himself, and we were merely waiters."

Because of his musical activities, the boy's classwork suffered and, as a result, he gave his parents many a heartache, for they were ambitious for their son. His father wanted him to become an educator, to teach his own people. Jimmy, on the other hand, had his own ideas of what he wanted to do. He wanted to be a musician, and nothing else seemed to satisfy him.

Eventually Bland finished the grade and high schools of Washington and went to Howard University. There he was in constant trouble because of his playing. He strummed and sang between classes; he strummed on his way from one building to another; he gathered boys and girls around him and staged concerts on the campus.

The professors at Howard didn't like this indifference to study; neither did his father. He feared his son would let his love of music interfere with scholarship, but Jimmy was no scholar and admitted it. It didn't seem to bother him to be told he was a dreamer and that no good could come of his activities.

On the other hand, those he entertained enjoyed his music and his carefreeness. His companions looked upon him as a man apart from others. They thought there was

an aura of a poet about him. Certainly his mind and soul were filled with melody. Music was his master.

He was seventeen at the time he tried to put on a musical show at the university. There again he met with opposition. The faculty refused to permit the show to go on, and he and his banjo were banned. Bland was told that if he wanted to sing, he should join the choir. Instead of joining the choir, he organized a minstrel show, and played one full week in a downtown hall without the faculty's discovering it. Out of that effort he made considerable money, the major portion of which he turned over to his mother.

This constant conflict between music and serious study actually made Jimmy begin to feel inferior. For a time, he believed he wasn't very bright. He passed through a period during which he was, in a sense, at war with the world. In arguments with his father, Jimmy's mother was usually the boy's champion, interceding gently on his behalf.

"That boy's *made* of music, Allen," she would insist. "He could no more stop playing than stop breathing. Maybe the old saying about square pegs in round holes has a lot of truth to it. Maybe his music can make as much of him as your studying will of you."

Allen Bland was a reasonable man, and more often than not would reply, "Maybe that's the way to look at it."

In Jimmy's mind, his mother was almost as strict as his father, though in a different way. Knowing that she did not completely share his father's viewpoint on music, he sensed that she knew what made the peculiar quirks in his character.

"Ma," he began, one afternoon upon his

return from his street-playing, "maybe some day I'll make up to you for all the trouble I've been. I just got the feeling that some day I *will* make up for it."

"Maybe you will, Jimmy," she replied, "but remember one thing. Even fun can be hard work."

"What you mean by that, Ma?"

"Just what I said. You like to play the banjo and sing. But if you just *play* at it, you won't amount to anything worth talking about. You got to work at anything— even fun—to be good at it."

The nation had entered a new phase in the entertainment field. Phineas T. Barnum, the greatest showman on earth, as he called himself, was exhibiting Lucifer, the fire-eater, the Siamese twins and the Peejee mermaid. The Barbary Coast was the attraction of the Far West, and what was over-looked in San Francisco, Chicago, and New York, where the Bowery was going full speed ahead, took place in Washington. Bland, as a young man, became part of this whirl of festivities.

It was not uncommon then for the President to leave the White House and walk over to Newspaper Row, a long line of one-story shacks on Fourteenth Street, just north of Pennsylvania Avenue, where a monument to American journalism, the National Press Building, now stands.

In the 70's, even Presidents had more liberties than they have now, guarded as they are every moment. They went to call on the correspondents and their bosses who came down from New York and as far away as Chicago for personal chats. Men such as "Marse" Henry Watterson, Charles A. Dana and Horace Greeley were frequent visitors. No matter how many celebrities were present, Bland and his banjo could always be found the center of attraction.

John Philip Sousa at that time played the violin in a music hall around the corner from Newspaper Row. In truth, the "Music Hall" was nothing more than an old-fashioned German beer garden, afterwards known as Gerstenberg's or the University of Gerstenberg's, where many notables got their degrees!

This was one of Bland's favorite spots, for it was his ambition to play his banjo there. Eventually he did, following in the foot-steps of the March King, who later became leader of the United States Marine Band. Later Sousa toured the world with his own band, and wherever he played a concert, he included the Bland melodies as encores.

Bland had matured by this time and was rated as a good dresser. Since he made enough money to buy his own good clothes, his family could raise no objections to his extravagance. Minstrel men in those days liked "loud" outfits, but Bland chose the quieter colors—blue, black, gray. With all his conservatism, he was known as a dandy by his followers. In that day statesmen wore boots under or over their trousers' legs; whereas Bland wore laced high shoes. When he entertained he wore dancing pumps, patterned after those designed for George Primrose, who had come to be a hero to the young man who was fast acquiring minstrel honors.

A slender young man, lithe of body, keen of mind, he looked as if he were always ready to go into his dance. He walked lightly and with a spring in his step, and as he grew into manhood, he developed a certain poise that remained with him always.

[28]

CHAPTER 6

SCHOOL DAYS

ITH HEAD ERECT AND HAIR neatly braided, a young girl walked into the classroom of Howard University with a group of other new pupils. Her bright eyes glanced over the room and nothing seemed to escape her attention.

Jimmy was aware of her from the first moment she appeared, and to the day of his death he could not have defined the reason for her influence over him, which began that day. She was not unusually attractive physically, although there was a quality that set her apart. One sensed in Mannie Friend a hidden strength like a deep, underground current. Perhaps Jimmy Bland recognized the motivating force of this current as he had felt the old Negro's music engulf him that autumn day in Philadelphia several years before.

Mannie had come in quietly with the other new pupils. She glanced at Bland briefly in passing, opened her book, and sat with her arms folded on the desk. His glance at her was equally brief, but for some reason that the boy did not then understand, he wanted to attract her attention.

From the very beginning she challenged him; she acted as a spiritual force over him, greater than that exerted by his parents.

He wanted to please her, and at the same time he resented this desire that she aroused in him. This battle in his own soul was to be the basis of many quarrels between the two of them in the years ahead.

Years later Bland admitted to his friend and colleague, Billy Kersands, that Mannie exercised a strange influence over him. She became almost as important to him as his music. That, as far as anyone knows, was the best way Bland could express his life-long relationship with Mannie Friend. And always, just as it had been that first day, it was more of a spiritual force with which she dominated him than it was a purely physical one. She, more than anyone in the world, had the power to make Jimmy Bland criticize himself. Through her eyes he felt as if he were gazing into a mirror that reflected his own weaknesses and imperfections.

When classes were over that afternoon, Jimmy Bland went to some effort to avoid the girl whose bright eyes had made such a deep impression on him. He would not even admit to himself a strong desire to find out more about her; he was conscious only of an impelling urge to hurry home. He even wanted to avoid his family, and was a trifle abrupt with his mother when she spoke to him.

As soon as he picked up his banjo he fled from the house for his usual engagement at Chamberlin's. That time he played and sang as he had never done before. The applause was even greater than usual, but the young troubadour scarcely noticed it. As he started home that night, he wanted to walk and walk, and to sing and play endlessly. He had never felt more alive. Gradually this restlessness passed, and he was content to sit in some quiet spot and think. After

wandering aimlessly for a while he found himself by the bank of the river. Here he seated himself on an upturned boat near an old pier. His eyes looked out into the darkness over the water, and he began to ponder on his school, the events of the morning, and the strange new girl who had entered the classroom and his life. Several hours passed before he finally arose and started toward home.

The next time he saw Mannie he became still more determined to make her acquaintance. Yet he was tongue-tied in her presence and couldn't even utter her name.

A short time after this Jimmy was walking home from college when he heard a rapid step behind him. He sensed who it was and began to walk a little faster. The steps broke into a run. There she was beside him, breathless, her eyes even brighter than he remembered them.

"Your name's Jimmy Bland, isn't it?"

"Yes, it is," he replied.

"They tell me you're quite a banjo player. They say you play beautifully."

With this praise, some of his shyness vanished; his eyes brightened and he slackened his pace, all the while striving to maintain his aloofness.

"Who says so?" he grinned.

"Some of the girls at school. They told me you play and sing at Chamberlin's." Her eyes were shining with an admiration that did not go unnoticed by Jimmy.

"Yes, I do. I play there just about every night."

"I think that's wonderful. I think it's the most wonderful thing."

"Shucks, it's not so much. Not as much as I'm going to do when I finish school."

"What are you going to do then?"

"I'm going to be a minstrel man and play and sing in theaters and maybe go to other cities—maybe to New York."

"Oh, my! Think of that!"

They were walking side by side now, Jimmy suiting his pace to hers.

"Your name's Mannie Friend, isn't it?"

"Yes. But I never told you. How do you know?"

"I've heard the teacher call on you, haven't I?" he asked a little testily. "No mystery about that. Say, you ever been in Lafayette Square?"

She replied that she had been there a few times.

"Well," he said, feeling extremely brave now, "I don't have to get to my job right away. How about if we walk through the square and maybe sit down for a while?"

They talked as they strolled over to the square, and they talked still more as they moved about the graveled walks and admired the statues and the seven-foot bronze vases on each side of the square.

"That statue weighs fifteen tons," Jimmy volunteered, referring to the Jackson figure. "It's one-third larger than life size. My father told me."

Then the conversation turned to Jimmy's father, and Mannie asked many questions about him. Jimmy had virtually told her the history of his family by the time they parted in front of Mannie's home.

"That was fine," the boy said. "I enjoyed talking to you. Hope I didn't talk too much about myself."

Mannie felt the feminine instinct arise within her. "Oh, no! Men ought to do the talking. They generally have more interesting things to say, anyhow."

In a sudden panic of embarrassment, Jimmy abruptly clapped on his hat and turned on his heel. Almost as quickly, he snapped around again.

"Say, Mannie, will it be all right if we walk home again tomorrow?"

"I'd like it a lot. And Jimmy, how about playing me some of your music sometime?"

"Oh, sure, sure." He waved to her, almost fiercely, and then turned and fled down the street.

At Chamberlin's that night for the second time he had no idea what he was playing. He saw the audience in front of him, and apparently he played as well as usual, for he heard the applause, but he could think of nothing but the girl across the aisle from him in the classroom and of his desire to see her again.

The dream persisted as he left the restaurant and returned home. He ate his supper in silence and went to bed immediately, but he did not go to sleep. For more than an hour Jimmy lay staring at the ceiling. It was strange. He had felt genuinely tired, but now he realized that instead of being sleepy he was intensely awake and more alert than he had been all day.

Suddenly he knew that he must get up and go out. He was soon into his clothes. Grabbing his banjo, he opened the window and slid down the rain pipe, just as he had done when he was a youngster.

As he moved rapidly away from the house, his fingers swept the strings gently and he began to sing one of those nameless songs that seemed to rise spontaneously from his own soul.

Without realizing it, he found himself retracing the route that he and Mannie had taken that afternoon. He continued through the square, past the bench where he and the girl had paused for a moment in their walk, still strumming on the banjo.

The next thing Jimmy knew, he was standing outside the neat little house in which Mannie Friend lived. The only wish he had at that moment was that she might appear without his summoning her, because she had sensed his presence. He wanted passionately to play for her; he wanted her to stand there beside him in the moonlight while he sang to her. At first he was bold enough to believe he could sing so forcefully that she would be sure to hear him. But he lost his courage and stood with the banjo at his side, looking at the house forlornly, while he tried to imagine which room might be hers.

The same impulse to run that had overcome him that afternoon returned. He was afraid that she might open the door, might come out and toward him. Again the youth turned and fled.

CHAPTER 7

BLAND THE YOUTH

ALMOST EVERY DAY AFTER THAT Jimmy and Mannie walked home from the college together. When the weather was good, they used to sit for a while either in Lafayette Square or at a particularly pretty spot on the bank of the Potomac. Jimmy usually played and sang, but sometimes they only talked, the conversation dwelling on his ambitions. Mannie would tell about her old home across the river in Virginia, and at such times her dark eyes would have a faraway look. Unlike Jimmy's family, Mannie's folks had not been free Negroes when she was born. Her grandmother still lived in a little cabin on what had been a thriving plantation before the war.

Even with Mannie, Jimmy was shy about performing his own works, as he was not yet sure of them, but as the days passed and he felt more and more at ease with her, he began to introduce his own music into his impromptu concerts. One afternoon, shortly after their first meeting, Jimmy allowed his fingers to glide over his banjo in one of his own compositions. The emotional strain of creating something for himself made him forget about Mannie momentarily.

"What are you playing now, Jimmy?" she asked quietly as she sat watching him.

He stopped playing and looked at her sulkily.

"Oh, just something I picked up."

"Must know what you're playing."

"I was just playing something that popped into my head, the way I've done before when there's nobody around."

"You mean you thought it up yourself? Out of your head?"

"Sure. What's so funny about that?"

"It's not funny, Jimmy; it's wonderful. I couldn't do it."

She leaned forward in her enthusiasm. "Jimmy, maybe you'll be a great man some day. Maybe you *will* be famous!"

"I'd like to make lots of money. I'd like to be a minstrel man. I like the way it feels to sing and play and have an audience clap at what I do. I'd like to be able to help out more with the family too."

Mannie's face looked a trifle sad.

"What's the matter?" he asked. "You're looking down in the mouth. What's wrong?"

"You'll get famous and you'll make lots of money—and then you'll forget all about me, Jimmy. I know that's what will happen."

"No, Mannie. I'll never forget you. You were the first person to care much about my music."

Jimmy took her hand and they started for home, just as the sun sank over the river behind them. Mannie was silent as they walked, and he could not cheer her up, no matter how hard he tried. It was strange, the feeling he had at that moment. He realized that during their talk about the future he had never once mentioned her in any of his plans. It was true that he was about twenty at this time and a college student, but it would have been only normal for him to have dreamed of their future together.

After another long silence, Mannie asked him whether he had ever written down any of his musical ideas.

"Wouldn't know how to, the way *they* do it," he said, referring to other composers. "I've sort of worked out a way to kind of remember for myself. But nobody else would know what I'd written down."

"But Jimmy, you must know how to write it down! It'll all be lost if you don't!"

"Oh, I guess I'll find a way sometime," he said. "Plenty of time for that."

The time was riper than Jimmy thought. He was still a student at Howard when he actually began to write music. One Saturday afternoon in the spring he was strumming his way to Mannie Friend's home for a walk along the Potomac.

As he often did when he was alone or thought himself alone, Jimmy sang and played the music that he really liked best— the music that he himself composed. As usual, that particular day he was paying little attention to his surroundings or to possible witnesses, as his fingers swept the strings and his youthful voice raised itself in song.

Suddenly he was interrupted by a deep, resonant voice.

"That's mighty nice music, son," it said. "Where'd it come from?"

Bland stopped playing and pressed his banjo under his arm. In front of him stood an old Negro, whose snow-white hair framed his gleaming brown face like a halo. Pressed down over the bushy white hair was a battered derby, which had taken on a green tinge with age and exposure to the weather. The man's bright eyes looked out from beneath bushy eyebrows that were as white as his hair. For all the worn appearance of his clothes, he gave the impression of a certain grandeur. The frock coat that covered him to his knees was visibly frayed, but it obviously had seen better days. In contrast, there was a heavy gold watch chain draped across a white vest that also showed signs of wear.

"Where'd you get it?" persisted the apparition, disrupting Jimmy's steady gaze.

"Oh, just somewhere," said Jimmy, overcome with embarrassment now.

"Just somewhere," the man repeated and came closer. "Well, I've been playing music a good many years and I never ran across that 'somewhere.' Mightn't be that you made it up, son?"

"Well, yes, I did," Jimmy stammered.

"What happens to it when you get through playing and singing it?" the old man asked, almost belligerently.

Jimmy shoved a pebble around with his foot.

"Oh, maybe I forget it, and maybe I do something if I like it very much."

"What might the 'something' be?"

"Well, I sort of mark it down a little so's I can remember how it went the next time I want to play it."

"You got some system of writing it down? Can anybody else read it?" There was excitement in the old man's voice.

"Oh, no!" Jimmy replied emphatically. The old man grunted.

"Ever hear of Stephen Foster?"

"Should say I have! His music's grand!"

"What you were playing sounded something like Foster. Not so polished as his, but . . ." He turned his silvery head to one side and squinted at the sky. "Well, it had something of the *feeling* of Stephen Foster.

It said the same sort of things in music. Understand?"

"Yes, sir," replied Jimmy meekly.

The old man regarded the young fellow solemnly for a moment before he spoke.

"How would you like to learn how to write down the notes? I mean, write 'em down so other people—maybe long after you're dead—can read 'em?"

"Oh, that would be wonderful!"

"All right, then. Come along with me."

Jimmy started to follow the old man; then he stopped.

"But . . ."

"But what?"

He suddenly remembered that he had been on his way to see Mannie. What would she do and say if he let her down this way without a word of notice? She lived quite a distance from the square, and there wouldn't be time for him to tell her the great news and then hurry back. In the meantime, the old man might change his mind, and it was unthinkable that Jimmy should miss an opportunity as rare as this.

"Oh, well," he decided to himself, "I can see her afterwards and explain."

"Nothing," he said aloud, as the old man stalked off in the direction of Pennsylvania Avenue.

Not another word was exchanged as the two walked along, Jimmy a pace or two behind the old man. The latter strode forward, humming softly to himself, and occasionally turning his head to appraise an unusually handsome carriage and pair dashing down the street. Bland felt a little miserable as he thought about Mannie sitting at home and waiting for him to take her on one of their regular Saturday afternoon excursions. Along with this sense of guilt was one of extreme excitement, for he could not help feeling that the old man was going to mean something very important to his future. What he didn't realize then was that his merely accompanying the old fellow instead of continuing to his meeting with Mannie constituted a pattern that was to endure throughout his life. Bland's music and his love of the wandering life of a minstrel were destined to be the great cleavage between the two.

At length the old man stopped in front of a poor lodging house, unlocked the door, and without seeming to pay any attention to Jimmy, stumped up the stairs to the third floor back, where he took out another key and opened a door. Only then did he turn around to admit Jimmy to the room. As he entered, he flung his hat on the single bed that stood by the only window.

"This is my studio," he announced with great dignity. "This, son, is where I write my own compositions and play them back to myself."

With a wave of his hand he indicated a battered music rack and an equally worn violin case.

"My name, son, is White," he began, opening his frock coat with a flourish and hooking his thumbs into the armholes of his vest. "They call me Professor White, because I'm not only a musician and a composer, but a teacher of music as well. I'm sixty years old and have been composing most of my life, but son, . . . What's your name, by the way?"

Jimmy told him.

"Son, I've never yet written anything that satisfied me . . . never anything that sounded as good as that little tune you were playing in the square."

Maintaining his superior attitude, he continued, scarcely pausing for breath, "Maybe I shouldn't tell you that. Maybe it'll go to your head. But, son, I think you've got the real thing. Mind you . . ." Here he tapped Bland on the shoulder. "It's nothing for *you* to be proud of. You had no more to do with it than the fact that you've got five fingers on each hand. It comes," he said reverently, "direct from God."

"Yes, sir," Jimmy answered politely, feeling called upon to say something and yet not knowing exactly how to reply.

"Don't interrupt me, son," continued Professor White. "Yes, from God. God gave that power to all the great composers, even to that same Stephen Foster we were discussing. Men like that are high priests of God's music. They have the gift. But," he wagged his finger admonishingly, "just because the gift is present, it doesn't mean that they don't have to work as hard as if they had no gift at all. Now, what I want to know is this . . ."

He paused again, and glared at the youth, who by this time was somewhat flabbergasted. This time he poked his finger at Jimmy's chest. "Are you willing to work? Are you willing to cultivate this fertile field that the Lord has given you? Are you willing to follow my instructions, and forego the pleasures of the flesh and give your best self to music?"

"Yes, sir," the boy replied. "I'd like to learn how to write down music the right way."

"That's what I like to hear and what I'll teach you, son, if you'll put yourself in my hands. Next Saturday I want you to come back at three sharp and we will begin. Now you may go. But remember what I said. I'm willing to give you my time. You must be

IN THE EVENING BY THE MOONLIGHT

willing—yes, you must be eager—to give me your time, and above all, your effort."

"Thank you, sir," was all Jimmy was able to say.

"Don't thank *me!*" thundered the professor. "Thank your Maker for the gift that He saw fit to give to you instead of to me."

Bland was so excited over his good fortune that he forgot all about his engagement to meet Mannie. He could hardly wait to get home to talk to someone about the great adventure that he was sure would be a turning point in his life. Rushing into the house, he poured out the whole story to his mother, who listened with an excitement she tried hard to conceal. When he had finished, she managed merely to caution him against believing everything Professor White told him.

"Mind you, I think it's wonderful that you're going to learn to write down the music, Jimmy. But he might not know too much about the difference between good and bad. So don't let it go to your head."

"I won't, Ma."

"Jimmy, Mannie was here looking for you. She said you'd promised to meet her. She was afraid you were sick."

"Oh! I didn't forget about meeting her. I just ran into this Professor White, and it seemed important to go with him."

Jimmy's conscience bothered him that evening, but by the time he went to bed he had managed to forget about his scheduled meeting with Mannie. Even after the lights were out, he talked to Ivanhoe about the glory of being able to put his musical thoughts on paper, just like a real composer.

"You mean it'll be just like regular reading and writing?" his brother inquired. "Will you show me when you can write some music down, Jimmy?"

Bland lay silent for a while, gazing into the darkness. "Show you! I'll show the whole world! I've *got* something! I just know I have!" He laughed softly.

Always ready to forgive, Mannie accepted Jimmy's explanation for his failure to meet her on Saturday, and soon they found themselves heading toward the Potomac.

Although she was usually content to let Jimmy do the talking, she became more loquacious than he had ever known her to be when he questioned her about her early life in Virginia. "It's beautiful, Jimmy," she sighed, "the most beautiful country you have ever seen. I wish sometime you could go there with me, down to the Tidewater Country. The plantation my people lived on was right on the James River, near Williamsburg. Oh, Jimmy, in the summer evenings all the colored folk would gather in front of one of the cabins in the moonlight. I will never forget those evenings in the moonlight."

Jimmy's fingers had been idly strumming the strings of the banjo as she talked. He softly hummed the last words she had spoken, to the accompaniment of the banjo.

"Mannie, listen!" His voice shook as he hummed softly:

"In the evening by the moonlight,
    You could hear those darkies singing."

Mannie was enthralled.

"Jimmy, it's beautiful. The words say just how I felt, but I couldn't express it that way. How I wish you could write the music! At least you can write down the words."

"Maybe I can write the music too," he boasted. "Just give me time."

CHAPTER 8

SONG IN HIS HEART

JIMMY BEGAN WORK IN EARNEST with Professor White, and the lessons became a regular part of Bland's life for several months. In the beginning, White had sensed that the youth had qualities that he himself had always dreamed of possessing. In a sense, he was living out a brief vicarious existence, realizing segments of his own early dreams, as he poured out his technical knowledge to the youth.

He was very strict, and after that first meeting, he never permitted himself to bestow even the slightest degree of praise. Perhaps he felt himself charged with a kind

of social responsibility. Actually, he was intensely aware of a professional pride. As Bland progressed in his studies, White grew more and more demanding. Once a week was not enough for the lessons, he soon decided. The boy had to come to the "studio" sometime during the day every day in the week.

It was clear—and very touching—that White's own musical career was drawing to an end, for despite his frequent assertions that demands for his talents as an interpreter were great, he seemed to have abundant time for Jimmy. Sometimes Bland suspected that the old fellow merely pretended engagements that forced his absence from the city for a day or two.

"Now, Jimmy," he would say, "just because I have to be out of town tomorrow and the next day, it doesn't mean that you're to loaf and take it easy. There's plenty of practicing that you can do."

With that he would fling open the door, raise his hands like a Roman emperor bidding farewell to a corps of ambassadors and depart. Jimmy wouldn't see him for a while. But it wasn't very long before the youth discovered the hollowness of those gestures. One evening on his way home from Chamberlin's, where he still played, he passed through the square. There he saw the familiar figure that had come to be almost a second parent to him.

The old man sat on a bench, but not as if he were merely pausing for a brief rest. His body, still swathed in its faded grandeur, was turned sideways, his head resting on an arm in an attitude that suggested despair. Jimmy's first instinct was to touch him and to ask whether anything was the matter. Then he remembered that his teacher was supposed to be out of town on an important musical engagement. The youth then realized that the only tactful thing to do would be to walk on, as if he had not seen him.

The next day, when he went back to the shabby room for his lesson, Bland found the old man noticeably less arrogant than he ever had been before. At the end of the session, he abruptly laid an arm across Jimmy's shoulder. He didn't look at the boy as he spoke, but kept his eyes on the floor as if he read some message there.

"Son, what I told you the first day I met you is true," he said in a low voice. "You've got a lot of ability. But life's a very tricky

thing sometimes. It's tricky like the ocean. No matter how good the ship is, God knows what can happen to it when the storm hits. And nobody knows what life can do to a talent like yours. Sometimes it's failure that destroys it; and more often than not, son . . ." He stopped, and his shining eyes seemed to probe at Bland's. "More often than not, Jimmy, success kills it off. Success can be like a sort of rot in your soul. You start worshiping the wrong gods and then, boy, like as not, you're lost."

"Son, success can lift a man to the heights or take him to poverty and disgrace, depending on the strength of the individual who has achieved it.

"You are the beneficiary of a gift that has been bequeathed to few men. If you do not make the most of it, if you fail to pass it on to your fellow men, then you are robbing your benefactor.

"It is within your hands and within the power of your mind to become an immortal. You can leave behind you an echo of divinity that has been denied to most of us. You have been given the power to create— a gift from God himself, and yet it in itself can destroy you as it has me and others before me."

As suddenly as he had begun, he stopped.

"I'll see you tomorrow, boy," he said abruptly, vaguely waving Bland out of the room. "See if you can write me a bit of new music."

During the time Bland took lessons from White, he continued to see Mannie, but the occasions were less and less frequent because of his devotion to his lessons with the old professor. At the same time he paid nothing but lip service to his classes at Howard. He didn't notice any change in Mannie at first, because he was so wrapped up in his ambition to master musical composition. But as time went on and his forgetfulness about little attentions grew more marked, Bland did observe a change in the girl.

She herself fought this change; she realized that she had no claim on him; she had no right even to think of claims where his music was concerned. But there were times when disappointment over his failure even to care about seeing her was too much for her to bear. On those occasions she became, at least within herself, all woman—a woman jealous of her man.

The weekly excursions to the river came almost to a complete halt, and Bland saw Mannie only for brief periods when he could escape from his bondage to White— a bondage that he loved passionately. Exulting in his growing ability to "write down" his musical thoughts, he talked of little else to Mannie when he saw her. But her strangeness upset him. He wanted to hold her friendship, perhaps not so much as she did his, but he knew that she meant a great deal to him.

One night after his regular engagement at Chamberlin's, the desire to see Mannie even overrode the weariness that had accumulated after a day of classes at Howard, a lesson with White, and also his performance at the restaurant. He had scarcely knocked on her door before it was opened, and Mannie was there to greet him. In her deep, throaty, lovely voice, she invited him into the house.

"No, Mannie, it is too beautiful a night to spend indoors. Let's go to Lafayette Square; there is something I want to talk to you about."

The park was only a few blocks away, so they soon found themselves seated on one of the benches facing the White House.

Jimmy, as always, had his banjo with him, and he started picking casually at the strings before he spoke.

"Mannie," he said, "how would you like to take me to see your grandmother in Virginia?"

Mannie's eyes sparkled. "I would love it, but how can we afford it?"

Jimmy's spirits sank. True, he had a few dollars saved, but not enough to travel all the way to the Tidewater with Mannie. For a moment Mannie was lost in thought.

"Jimmy," she cried, "I know a man who was the overseer on our folks' plantation who is in Washington. He's just delivered a load of tobacco, and he plans to return home the day after tomorrow. I am sure he would be glad to take us with him on the return trip."

"Mannie, that would be wonderful! Can we see him tonight?"

"Could be; he stopped in to see us last night. He's staying at the Willard Hotel."

Jimmy picked up his banjo and started to pluck the strings, accompanying the music with words that he had composed a short time before. After he had played the song through, Mannie asked him to play two or three of her other favorites.

As Jimmy finished his last song, both he and Mannie were startled at the sound of a voice, for they thought they were alone. Neither of them had noticed the man sitting on a bench behind them.

"Son, you can really handle that banjo. The songs you played are new to me, and yet I am in the show business. Thought I knew all the popular hits Who composed those?"

Jimmy hesitated. "I did, sir."

"You mean you actually composed that music and wrote the lyrics too?"

"Yes, sir," Jimmy replied.

"Son, you really have music in your heart. That was beautiful. My name is John Ford, owner of Ford's Theatre. Why don't you drop in and see me sometime? I think we can use some of your talent."

John Ford! Jimmy had often gone to the Ford Theatre to hear the minstrels. And now to meet the man who owned Washington's number one theater was surely a great moment, and moreover to play for him, was overwhelming.

"Thank you, sir. I would like to very much. Do you really think there would be any part for me?"

"Can't tell what we might work out, but I would like to have you meet George Primrose."

"George Primrose!" Jimmy felt as if he were walking on air. To think of meeting his idol, the great minstrel.

"Thank you, sir," was all Jimmy could say. Then he added quickly, "I'm going away this week, but I will surely see you after I come back."

The boy and girl watched Ford walk away before they spoke.

Then Jimmy asked softly, "Did you hear what he said, Mannie?"

"Yes, Jimmy, I heard. Here is your chance to have your songs heard. And yet it makes me afraid—afraid that there is something between us, something that will always keep us apart. It is almost like sharing you with another woman. I guess I'll never really have you to myself."

"What other woman?" he demanded roughly.

Mannie laughed. "Not really another woman, Jimmy. I mean the music is like a rival. It makes you different; it makes it seem as if there is a part of you that never will belong to anyone."

For a long time Jimmy was silent and lonely. For the first time he realized that he was different from other people. He knew that in his desire to create he would have to forfeit much. It is possibly true that this moment was a definite turning point in James Bland's life. Here for the first time his path and Mannie's started in different directions.

"Oh, Mannie," he said when he came out of his reverie, "I couldn't stand it if I lost you."

"You won't lose me, Jimmy, but I will lose you. I'll lose you the same way all other women will lose you. They will lose you to your music. Jimmy, you have so much song in your heart that it will always separate us."

Mannie spoke in a solemn tone, perhaps without being fully aware that her words were prophetic. James Bland was to become acquainted with many women in his lifetime. None of them influenced him to the extent that Mannie had, but not one of them ever divorced him from his music.

Mannie pressed his hand, but it did not seem to affect Jimmy. He felt that he was on an island by himself. He was lost—lost in a feeling of loneliness. He felt condemned to a state of being that he had not chosen. He could not talk, he was overcome with a feeling of self-pity for his lot. Why, oh, why, could he not be like other people!

"Mannie," he finally blurted out, "let's go home, and tomorrow we will see that man about going to Virginia."

M·LARER

CHAPTER 9

A SONG IS BORN

JOHN MACGREGOR HAD ALWAYS BEEN a favorite with the Negro slaves on the plantation in Virginia where Mannie had been born. Although he was a fair and kindly man, she remembered him as stern and demanding in protecting his employer's interests. He had never been known to abuse or mistreat a slave; likewise he had never tolerated laziness on the part of the workers. It was believed that he was an abolitionist at heart, but he had never rebelled against or questioned the system of enforced servitude. He knew he was living in the midst of a dying aristocracy, and that time was running out.

His Scotch instinct told him that when the apple was ripe it would fall, and the feudal system that prevailed had long since become more of a liability than an asset to the South. Had not his own country stamped out this evil traffic in human souls some forty odd years before?

In spite of his personal feelings, John MacGregor simply accepted the status quo and demanded a full day's work from everyone under him. When the war came, Judge White, the owner of the plantation, and his only son secured commissions under General Longstreet in the Army of Northern Virginia. They were quite content to leave

the running of the plantation in Mac-
Gregor's capable hands, knowing that he
would carry on to the best of his ability and
look out for the owner's interests.

Even during the dark days when the
Union troops invaded the Tidewater, Mac-
Gregor was able to plant and harvest his
crops. His canny Scotch instinct to provide
for the future stood the family in good stead
when the war was over. While the other
planters were shipping all their cotton to
Richmond to bolster the rapidly declining
Confederacy, MacGregor always managed
to withhold enough to insure seed for the
following spring planting. Consequently,
when the war was over and the old judge
and his son failed to return, Mrs. White
and her sister had their overseer to thank
for being far less destitute than many of
their neighbors.

After the war most of the Negroes left
the plantation, with the exception of the
older folk who had never known any other
home and who had no desire to find one.
Among these was Mannie's grandmother.
When Mrs. White and MacGregor assured
her and the other erstwhile slaves that they
could remain in their cabins and would be
paid for their services, the old people were
very grateful.

Both of Mannie's parents had been house
servants in the White household, and Mac-
Gregor remembered the girl as a quiet child
of six or eight—a great favorite of Judge and
Mrs. White.

When she asked him to take her and
Jimmy down into Virginia to her old home,
he seemed glad to do it. He told her that he
would pick them up at the corner of Pennsylvania Avenue and Seventeenth Street at
five o'clock the next morning. Both Mannie

and Jimmy were waiting there when his
heavy farm wagon drove into sight.

"Climb in, lass," MacGregor boomed.
"And is this the lad you've been telling me
about? What is the instrument you're
luggin' under your arm, lad?"

"It's a banjo, sir," replied Jimmy as he
helped Mannie climb up, and then he
pulled himself up onto the seat after her.

"This is Jimmy Bland. You should hear
him play, Mr. MacGregor. He really makes
music."

"Aye, 'tis good for a man to make music.
Your people have used song to take them
over many a weary mile. 'Tis a long mile we
have to go too." He flecked the horses lightly
with his whip and turned down Seventeenth
Street, heading for Constitution Avenue.
They had timed the trip so as to catch the
ferry that would take them to Alexandria,
and no sooner had MacGregor driven the
team aboard than the ferry pulled out.

As a boy Bland had been well acquainted
with poverty, but after his family had moved
to Washington and his father had found a
good job, Jimmy was in much better circum-
stances. He was therefore unprepared for
the squalor and sordid wretchedness that he
saw as they approached the western bank of
the Potomac. Dilapidated houses, spread out
along the bank, marked the beginning of the
Negro settlement. Dark and filthy junk
shops reeking with vile smells, the rotting
quay lapped by the quiet waters of the
Potomac, aroused in him a sense of utter
revulsion.

Jimmy was a product of the North despite
the fact that his forbears were originally
from the Deep South. City-born and city-
bred, his contact with rural life had been
remote, so the first glimpse of the conditions

[45]

under which his people lived filled him with sadness.

The paddle wheel was thrown into reverse, churning up the water in the stern, as the ferry glided into its slip. The blocks were removed from behind the rear wheels of the farm wagon, and MacGregor gave the whip to the grays, urging them off the ferry and up the sharp incline toward the center of Alexandria.

It was not long before they were out of the poorer section along the river and on Cameron Street. Always sensitive to his surroundings, Bland's mood soon changed, and he began to enjoy the beauty of the stately houses and lovely gardens as they approached the better sections of the old town.

Jimmy drew in his breath at the grandeur of the old Fairfax house that had been built of brick brought over from England by one of the early members of the family. His pleasure turned to sadness as he remembered that the Fairfaxes no longer lived there, having been scattered by the ravages of war.

As they drove by the old Carlisle House, or Mansion House, as it was then called, MacGregor told them that it was there the British Council met with General Braddock, who later invited young Major Washington to join his ill-fated march to western Maryland.

MacGregor planned to change horses in Fredericksburg, having left his own team there on the way up to Washington. By changing horses, and by driving from early morning until late at night, he hoped to be in Richmond the second night of the trip.

Neither Jimmy nor Mannie was ever to forget this long journey. The heavy farm wagon had not been built for passengers,

and the dusty road, with its deep ruts, did not add to their comfort. As the September sun rose higher in the sky, the heat became almost unbearable.

In order to relieve the monotony of the trip, Jimmy played and sang several songs, and after much coaxing on Mannie's part, the old Scotchman was also persuaded to sing one of his favorite Highland ballads. Jimmy was as pleased with MacGregor's songs as the old Scotsman was with Jimmy's. Finally Jimmy suggested that all three of them sing some of Stephen Foster's songs. It was a strange sort of harmony, that blending of Scotch dialect and the deep rich tones of the two young Negroes.

When they left Fredericksburg the next morning Jimmy was conscious of something different about the country through which they were passing. For the first time in his life he saw cotton and sweet potatoes growing in the fields. True, the corn fields looked almost the same as they did in the North, but the Negroes' cabins dotting the landscape formed an entirely different picture. Jimmy became very quiet and was engrossed in his own thoughts.

For miles they rode along silently, then Mannie finally spoke. "I have dreamed of coming back to old Virginny ever since we left, and now I can scarcely believe we are almost home. Isn't it beautiful, Jimmy? Just wait until you see the river; you will love the Tidewater and the plantation."

Jimmy was amused by her enthusiasm. Yet, as he closed his eyes, and leaned back in the seat, a feeling of mellowness stole over him. No doubt it was at that moment that James Bland fell in love with the state of Virginia.

The farm wagon and its occupants arrived

in Richmond after nine o'clock that night. Mr. MacGregor decided it would be best if they stayed there overnight. By getting an early start in the morning, they would be able to reach the plantation by noon. Mannie knew some friends from the Tidewater who were living in Richmond and who were glad to have the young people stay with them. It was agreed that MacGregor would pick them up early the following morning.

The route they took from Richmond brought them to the Forge. From there they cut south to Charles City, which was only nine miles from the White plantation.

From the Forge on, the country was much greener than it had been north of Richmond, due to the fact that they were on a peninsula between the James and York Rivers. Also, the tidewater inlets acted as a series of irrigation canals that kept the soil moist at all times.

They drove into a heavily wooded area over a corduroy road with a bog on each side. Several times they noticed a ripple in the black water of the bog caused by a turtle or a moccasin snake, which, alarmed by their approach, sought the sanctuary of the swamp waters.

Jimmy had never heard so many birds singing. Some he recognized by their trill, but there was one whose tone had haunted him from the time they had entered the forest. He had never known that a bird's song could inspire him the way this one did. It's trill was not always the same. At times he would think that he recognized the rolling syllables of the robin, only to hear it change into the trill of a scarlet tanager. Before he could reach any conclusion the notes would change into a burst of song entirely different

from anything he had ever heard. One time when this had happened, he heard the plaintive call of a loon in the distance. Much to his amazement, the warbling of the songbird that had puzzled him for so long, ended abruptly and from the same direction he heard an echo of the loon.

He thought at last that he could identify the bird. Turning to Mannie he said, "Did you hear that second loon just then?"

"That wasn't a loon, Jimmy, it was a mocking bird."

He smiled, "I thought so, but it really had me puzzled. No wonder they have written songs about that bird."

Once they left the corduroy road and swamp they were on firmer ground. Cypress trees gave way to oak saplings and as suddenly as they had entered the swampwoods, they left it behind and entered open country—open country such as Jimmy had never before seen. On one side of the road was an unbroken field of cotton in full bloom; on the other side stretched field after field of waving green cornstalks, their golden tassels waving gently in the breeze. The beauty of the Virginia countryside overwhelmed Jimmy. Even Mannie's enthusiastic description of it had not done it justice.

MacGregor waved his whip in a semi-circle, " 'Tis the Whites' fields you're seein' " he said proudly. "Won't be long now."

Soon they came to a long lane, bordered on each side by huge sycamore trees. The team turned in here, and presently a large Georgian red brick house came into view.

The White plantation was one of the oldest farms in the Tidewater country, the house having been built in the early part of the eighteenth century, shortly after the capital of colonial Virginia had been moved to Williamsburg. Like most of the buildings of its day, it had been built for comfort and utility. Its broad smooth lawns shaded by huge black oaks gave it an atmosphere of strength and permanence.

Following the drive around to the back of the house, MacGregor drove the team up to the stables. Mannie and Jimmy climbed down from the wagon and Mannie led Jimmy along a path down toward the river and her grandmother's cabin.

She was waiting for them in the doorway —a little old lady with stooped shoulders and snow-white hair. She greeted Mannie fondly and then turned her sharp black eyes on Jimmy. Mannie had written to her about her friend, knowing that Mrs. White would read the letter to her. Naturally, her grandmother was anxious to meet this boy who seemed to mean so much to Mannie. It did not take the old lady long to make up her mind that she liked him, but she also sensed something strange about him—something that set him apart. Without knowing the reason for it, she felt that he could never bring happiness to Mannie.

That afternoon Jimmy and Mannie strolled down to the river, where they sat down on the bank, their backs against a sycamore. A great sense of contentment swept over Jimmy as he gazed out over the river.

Jimmy pulled a piece of paper and a pencil from his pocket and handed them to Mannie. "Mannie," he said, "I've had something in my mind ever since we left Alexandria. I remember your saying you had dreamed of being carried back to old Virginny. Up until now I haven't been able to put the thoughts into words. Now I can hold them no longer."

He picked up his banjo, strummed the strings slowly, and started to sing the words of "Carry Me Back to Old Virginny." Mannie took the pencil and started to write.

Neither of them realized that the song born that day on the bank of the James River was to become Bland's greatest composition.

HAVERLY'S MASTODON MINSTRELS

CHAPTER 10

BACKSTAGE

ONE OCTOBER DAY IN 1874, GEORGE Primrose, minstrel man and greatest soft shoe dancer of his time, had just left the stage of the old Ford Theatre in Washington. The deafening applause he had received after his performance still rang in his ears.

Returning to the footlights, he took another bow, but the audience was not satisfied with this. Three times he had to return to give an encore, to dance to the strains of "Swanee River," one of the favorite tunes of the day. Finally the audience left the theater, and John Ford came to the star's dressing room.

"There's a young man outside who would like to see you," he told the minstrel.

"What for?" Primrose asked.

"He says he wants to join the show," replied Ford.

Primrose kicked off a dancing pump with annoyance. "Listen, John," he pleaded, "I have no time to waste on young hopefuls. Billy West and I are quitting Skiff and Gaylord's Minstrels to go with Colonel Jack Haverly as a team. He is going to give us top billing as Primrose and West."

"Congratulations, George! That'll be some team; the greatest in minstrel history, if I'm any judge.

"But it won't take you a minute to see this boy. Give him a chance. He's been waiting all through the show for you. Maybe you'll find you want to take him along with you. Honestly, George, I think he really has talent. I wish you would see him at least."

"What's his specialty, selling songbooks?" Primrose asked facetiously.

"He writes songs," replied Ford, pretending not to notice Primrose's banter. "I met him the other night in Lafayette Square after hearing him play the banjo and sing a song that sounded to me like a natural."

Primrose kicked off his other pump as he wiped the burnt cork off his face. "A friend of yours, John? How old is he?"

"I never saw him before," answered Ford. "But I do know his father, who is a clerk in the Patent Office. The young fellow is a student at Howard University, and he looks about nineteen or so. His father is also taking a postgraduate course in law there."

"Did you say Harvard?" Primrose wasn't quite sure whether he had heard correctly.

"No, Howard. You know—it's the new government school for Negroes here in Washington."

Primrose rubbed the last bit of black from his face before he spoke. "Is he colored?"

"Yes, he is, but let me bring him in, anyhow."

"It's no use, John. It would just be wasting his time and mine."

"Why do you say that?"

"You know why just as well as I do," explained Primrose patiently. "Here we are, all blacked up with burnt cork to look like Negroes, but we can't have a real colored man in our show." A tinge of bitterness crept into his voice. "John, these people have music in their soul. They've given us the Negro spirituals, which have become part of this country's music. In spite of this, we're not far enough advanced in our thinking to admit this by placing him in our show. Why doesn't he try Haverly's colored minstrels? They'd take him on. I'll give him a letter to my new boss. That's the best I can do."

"No, it isn't. This boy's been watching your act at almost every performance, and I'm not going to disappoint him. You've got to talk to him, even if you can't do anything else. I'm going to bring him in. He idolizes you."

Like most troubadours, Primrose could not resist this flattery. "Okay, let's see what he looks like," he shouted, as Ford headed for the wings.

Within a few moments Ford returned, accompanied by young Bland, his banjo tucked in its customary place under his arm.

Jimmy was obviously nervous as Ford introduced him to the great minstrel, but it wasn't long before he felt at ease.

"Sit down, son," said the star. "I see you brought your joy box with you. What can you do with it?"

"I pick at it a little, sir," the lanky youth whispered modestly.

"He does better than that," his sponsor bragged. "Let's hear that song I heard you play the other night over in Lafayette Square."

Jimmy ran his fingers over the strings of the banjo, his eyes looking straight at Primrose. The plaintive melody of "In the Evening by the Moonlight" soon echoed through the room.

"That's nice music, son. I never heard it before. Whose melody is it?"

CARRY ME BACK TO OLD VIRGINNY

"I made it up myself sometime ago."

"Did you write any lyrics for it? Can you sing the words?"

"Yes, sir," Jimmy strummed a few more chords, and then began to sing the song that he had composed with Mannie's help as they strolled along the Potomac in the moonlight.

"That's great! I'd like to hear that again, but can you play 'Swanee River'?" asked Primrose. "It's the song that I dance to quite a lot."

"I know. I've seen you dance many times, Mr. Primrose. Every time I get a chance I get a ticket in the gallery of this theater."

"Why do you want to be a minstrel, Jimmy?" asked Primrose, both flattered and impressed by the boy's sincerity.

"Because," and Jimmy paused, "because I think it is a privilege to be able to entertain people. I think that it is the greatest thrill on earth. But you asked me to play 'Swanee River' for you. Before I do that, will you let me play and sing something I composed the other day when I was down in Virginia?"

"By all means, son, let's hear it."

Once again Bland put his banjo in position, idly picked a few chords by way of introduction. Then he began to strum gently the notes of a song that was destined to take its place among the nation's all-time favorite folk music.

When he finished, Primrose smiled. "Nice melody," he agreed briefly. "Now let's hear the words."

Jimmy sat down on a near-by chair, tilted it back against the wall, and closed his eyes.

He sang softly at first; the rich young voice grew in volume as the boy gained confidence.

"Carry me back to old Virginny,
There's where the cotton and the corn and 'tatoes grow,
There's where the birds warble sweet in the springtime,
There's where this old darkey's heart am long'd to go.
There's where I labored so hard for old Massa,
Day after day, in the field of yellow corn,
No place on earth do I love more sincerely
Than old Virginny, the state where I was born."

For a moment after Jimmy ended his song, the room was hushed. Bland raised his head and looked at the two men. Tears welled up in Ford's eyes. Primrose was speechless with amazement. All his life he had heard plantation melodies, but never before had he known one that affected him like this one. At last he found his voice.

"You wrote that song?" he demanded. "Sounds like Stephen Foster to me. It's got everything in it that he put into his music."

The youth started to place the banjo in its case. His eyes lighted with pleasure at the compliment. "Stephen Foster is my favorite composer," he replied simply.

"Don't put that thing away," the minstrel shouted. "Play that song again."

Bland turned to Ford.

"Go ahead, Jimmy," said the theater manager. "I want to hear it again just as much as he does."

Once again the plaintive melody echoed through the dressing room and penetrated even to the backstage area, for Jimmy played and sang more loudly this time. Doors opened, as one by one the members of the minstrel troupe left their own rooms to hear the lilting music of a new song. In hushed groups they stood, thrilled by a song they instinctively recognized as a great piece of music.

On Primrose's and Ford's insistence Bland played and sang the song again and again. Finally, the entire troupe joined in the chorus, and the words of "Carry Me Back to Old Virginny" reverberated to the rafters of the theater.

An hour before curtain time for the evening show Primrose permitted Bland to stop playing. By that time he knew all about Professor White and the help he had given Jimmy.

At first Primrose had been suspicious of the originality of Bland's compositions, for he had detected in them a similarity to Foster's style. What he did not realize, however, was that Stephen Foster and James Bland were spiritual brothers. One was white, the other Negro, but both had the same spark of genius. Bland, like Foster, he finally realized, had captured the Negro pattern, and neither could have kept himself from expressing this any more than he could have stopped a raging torrent.

Stephen Collins Foster had died only ten years before in New York City, at the early age of thirty-eight. His songs had set a tempo and had created a fashion. No one had come along to supplement his album until the advent of Bland.

When the last notes from Jimmy's banjo had died away, Primrose jumped to his feet. He grabbed the boy's hand. "Young man," he said, "I can't put you in our show, but better still, I can use your song."

"You mean you will really take my song?"

"Take your song?" echoed Primrose.

"Son, that song will rouse the nation. Better than that, the people will take you to their hearts after they hear 'Carry Me Back to Old Virginny.' "

All this time Ford was watching the procedure eagerly and inwardly delighted with his own discovery of a young genius.

"Look here," he said, "we'd better get down to business. We're not going to make any mistakes in the way we put this song across. What's the first step, George?"

"I'll have it orchestrated, and we'll open with it in Baltimore next Monday night," said Primrose. "Now I've got to get moving if I'm to put on a show tonight."

Young Bland and Ford walked out through the stage alley together.

"I sure appreciate what you've done for me, Mr. Ford," Bland said in a trembling voice. "I don't know what I'd have done without your help."

"Forget it, son! That song would have made its way without me, don't worry. Now you go home, Jimmy, and get the manuscript. Bring it here; then we'll tell you what to do."

The youth hurried home, too excited to do more than snatch a bit of food as he told his parents what had happened, then dash back to the theater with the manuscript.

"The first thing we must do is to make a copy for Primrose. Then we'll send the original to the Library of Congress for copyrighting," Ford told him.

The copy Bland made with a rough-edged ruler was crude, but it was sufficiently good, for Primrose to use, as Ford commented, "He's heard the song so much by now, he must know it almost by heart!"

That night after the audience poured out of the theater after the performance Ford took the young composer to the minstrel's dressing room.

"Got that song for me?" Primrose demanded.

Bland handed the copy to him and waited for the minstrel's reaction.

"Did you make any changes in it?" he inquired, scanning the music eagerly.

"A note here and there."

"Let's hear it again."

As he finished, a short, jovial-looking man came in and sat down and was introduced as Billy West.

Again Bland was ordered to render the song for the newcomer's benefit.

"Good," was West's only remark. This laconic reply disappointed Jimmy somewhat, for he wanted everybody to love his song.

"Good!" shouted Primrose. "It's great! We'll knock 'em in the aisles with this thing! We're opening in Baltimore with it Monday night."

"Don't be foolish," West warned him. "Wait till we join Haverly. Why waste it? He'll go for that song."

"He can get it later. It'll be worth that much more to him by that time."

A harvest moon shone over the city as Bland walked slowly homeward. He was dazed by the suddenness of his success. He had known instinctively that this song was the best he had composed, but he had never supposed that it would be on its way to fame within a few months after its composition. At the same time his mind had never been so full of ideas. He wanted to talk to someone, but he knew that his family would have been in bed for hours. He also realized that Mannie, too, would be asleep, so he decided that the person he really wanted to talk to was Professor White. The old fellow kept unorthodox hours; perhaps he would be up and could see him.

As the youth turned down Pennsylvania Avenue to the "studio," he thought of the reception White had given the song when Jimmy had first shown it to him a few days after he had returned from Virginia. The old professor had scrutinized the music intently for a few minutes; then with a loud "harumph!" which served to conceal his excitement, he had reached for his violin and played the song, occasionally glowering at Bland.

"Well, son," he said as he drew the bow across on the last note, "all I can say is that you've done something that I think is wonderful." He brooded a moment. "Let's see, Jimmy. You're not twenty years old yet and you've written what, in my humble opinion, is a great song. Don't go rushing out right away to try to sell it or get it performed. I can't tell you just why, but that's my instinct. Write some more songs while you're in the mood. Always remember that your greatest happiness will come from the writing. If it happens that applause gives you more pleasure, be careful. Anyhow, son, there's nothing else for me to teach you. You know enough for your purposes, and you'll learn more from yourself than you would from me. Good-by and God bless you."

The afternoon of the rehearsal of his song Bland sat alone in the darkened theater as Primrose and a talented trio sang "Carry Me Back to Old Virginny." The youth was silent as the realization of what the future had in store for him swept over him. This was the life he must follow, and for the first time in his existence he knew that all his dreams would come true. For Bland there could never be a more beautiful scene than the one being enacted on the stage at that moment.

"Just let me keep on being able to write music," he prayed as the manager clapped him on the shoulder.

"How does it sound to you now, young fellow?" asked Ford.

"Sounds good to me," was all the composer could reply about the most dramatic moment in his life.

But to Mannie, whom he visited after the rehearsal, he was more expansive. "I'm in!" he cried. "They think it's as good as we did. Mannie, my song's going to be famous, and maybe some day I'll be rich."

"I knew they'd like it," she whispered.

He looked at her narrowly. "You sound sad about it."

"No. No, I can't be sad, Jimmy. Not now."

"What do you mean . . . you can't be sad?"

She hesitated. "I couldn't let myself be sad. You belong to the whole world now, Jimmy. You'll never belong to me nor any other girl."

"Don't cry, Mannie," he pleaded, seeing tears in her eyes. "There's nothing to cry about just because people like the song we wrote. Mannie, the thing that's important is that night we composed it and the way we felt . . . so sort of like belonging to each other."

"No, Jimmy. I must try to think of you the way I think of that night, as something to look at and enjoy, but not to own. It makes me sad and happy all at the same time. It makes me happy because I can hope that I had something to do with creating your masterpiece."

Jimmy was upset. He didn't really understand what she meant.

"Oh, Mannie," was all he could say, "I'm just happy that they like our song."

"You said 'our' song again. You said it the other night too."

"Sure it's our song. You were with me when it happened."

" 'Happened!' " she echoed. "What a way to say it! But Jimmy, I had no more to do with it than . . . But anyhow, it'd make me happy to think of it that way. Our song," she murmured, biting her lips. "The one thing that's Jimmy Bland that I can keep forever."

CHAPTER 11

THE MINSTREL MAN

T HE PREMIÈRE OF "CARRY ME Back to Old Virginny" took place in Baltimore, Maryland, on Monday after Bland had played the song for Primrose and Ford in the theater. Its success was immediate, and before long it became popular in Washington.

Bland's reputation as an entertainer had grown by this time. He was in constant demand throughout Washington.

Even though his parents still objected to his becoming a professional entertainer, he eventually persuaded them that this was his career.

One of the places where he appeared regularly was Harvey's Restaurant, one of the most famous dining rooms in the city, at the corner of Eleventh Street and Pennsylvania Avenue, where the Department of Justice now stands. This was the meeting place of the old Canvasback Club, forerunner of the present-day Gridiron Club.

It was in Harvey's that Bland wrote, composed and tried out the music and lyrics for his songs at the annual dinners of the Club, which, like the Gridiron Club, had no regular clubroom of its own. In this he was encouraged by Tom Harvey, who wanted his restaurant to become as well-known as

Chamberlin's, and thereby he became one of Bland's early sponsors.

It has been said of Tom Harvey that had he not gone into the restaurant business he would have become a showman. He knew all the leading show people of Washington of the 70's, he had seen and heard all the great artists of the concert hall, and so when the young composer came along, Harvey was quick to recognize a real find in him.

Harvey staged private parties in a second-floor room over his restaurant. It was at one of these affairs that Bland first played publicly "In the Evening by the Moonlight." The restaurateur recognized the song as a hit, and arranged to have Bland play and sing it in December before the hundred members of the Canvasback Club.

President Grover Cleveland had belonged to the Club even before he had gone to the White House to serve his first term. The beloved General Robert E. Lee had also long been a member.

Thus Cleveland had the opportunity to hear James Bland sing and play "Carry Me Back to Old Virginny" and "In the Evening by the Moonlight." The future President was very enthusiastic about Bland and his music.

It was the custom at the Canvasback Club, after the members had completed their ritual, eaten a superb dinner that could not, according to the gourmets, be duplicated today for one hundred dollars per plate, to sit back, relax, throw their napkins on the table and listen to songs.

Bland and his banjo became so popular that he appeared there each year he happened to be in Washington, even after he had started his stage career. Sometimes he would test his new songs on the members.

While he was usually assured of a kindly and sympathetic audience, they could also be highly critical.

If the song made a hit, they did not hesitate to tell him, and so Bland was reasonably certain that if it were successful there, it would be elsewhere.

Bland played at private dinners and at weddings among his own people as well as at affairs staged by the white population, among whom he had many friends. Since he was descended from a line of deeply religious people, it was natural that a note of spirituality crept into some of his compositions. "Oh, Dem Golden Slippers," another of his popular songs, was actually inspired while he was playing at a wedding, although the words had been carried in his mind for many years. Some of his other compositions, notably, "Heaven Is My Harbor," "Keep Dem Golden Gates Wide Open," "In the Morning by the Bright Light," have a spiritual significance.

A versatile, as well as a prolific writer, he could always adjust himself to the occasion, and although he did compose some spirituals, he seemed fonder of the popular style of music. He turned out his songs so fast that many were never copyrighted, and in some cases they appeared later under the name of another composer. Bland is accredited with having composed over seven hundred melodies, although only thirty-eight of his songs are filed in the copyright division of the Library of Congress.

One of the composer's great admirers was the late Victor Herbert. Shortly after he had arrived from his native Ireland, where his grandfather had written the popular ditty, "The Low Backed Car," Herbert became acquainted with Bland's music.

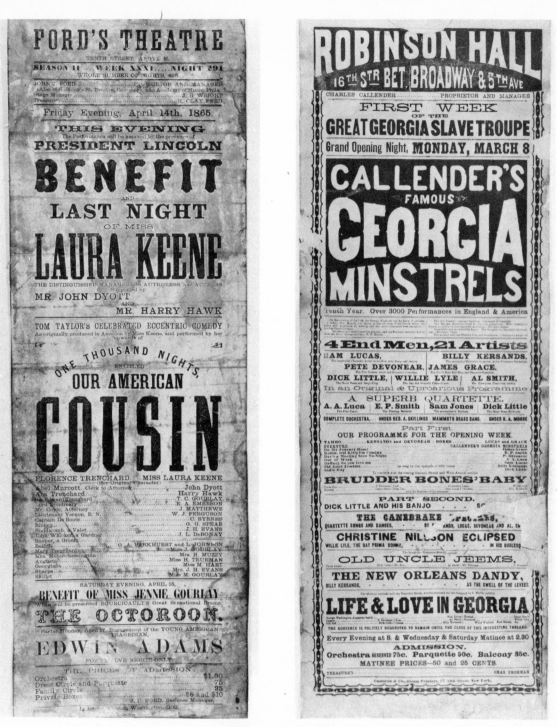

From the playbill collection at Keen's English Chop House, New York City.

Two playbills of James Bland's day. Left: Historic Ford's Theatre poster of program the night of President Lincoln's assassination. Right: Billy Kersands is featured as "the unequalled plantation humorist" on a Georgia Minstrels' playbill.

Herbert was with a symphony orchestra at the National Theatre as a cello player when he first became acquainted with Bland's songs and melodies. One feature on the musical program of that theater was an elaborate arrangement of "Carry Me Back to Old Virginny." The music intrigued Victor Herbert.

"This Stephen Foster certainly knew how to compose," Herbert remarked to Theodore Thomas, conductor of the orchestra.

"That's right; he was the soul of music," acknowledged Thomas.

" 'Carry Me Back to Old Virginny' has a haunting melody."

Thomas shook his head. "Foster didn't write that song. It was written by a young colored fellow here in Washington. He's a friend of Harry Rapley's, the manager of the National. You must have heard of him— James Bland, the Negro minstrel."

Herbert was skeptical. "A colored man wrote that? If he did, then an Irishman is going to write more of that kind of American music."

Ever since Bland had talked to George Primrose, he thought about the minstrels, and when he finally decided to join a company he approached Colonel Jack Haverly, whose troupe was playing in Baltimore. There the two men reached an agreement, and the would-be minstrel joined the ranks of the Haverly Colored Minstrels.

Bland had a great deal to learn about minstrelsy, but he worked into the routine gradually. At first he had only a minor part in the dress circle, and he sang only in the opening and closing choruses with the entire company. Later he was given a character bit to do at the end of the first act; and in the second act he was permitted to play a banjo solo. To him this was his greatest achievement, and it wasn't long before Bland and his banjo were on the way to fame and glory.

By the end of his first season with Haverly, he was permitted to sing some of his own compositions—sometimes "Carry Me Back to Old Virginny," sometimes "In the Evening by the Moonlight," accompanied by a quartet, and occasionally, "Oh, Dem Golden Slippers." Those were the three tunes that he considered his favorites. And to add to his already hard-won laurels, he was billed as their author and composer.

For many years Negro minstrels were not permitted in the professional theater. The end men, Mr. Bones and Mr. Sambo, as well as the fellow members of the troupe, were white men, their faces blackened with burnt cork. But the innate sense of humor, the love of laughter, and the rhythm of the Negro people had set the pattern for the minstrel show itself, which for almost fifty years was the most popular form of entertainment in America. When Negroes were eventually admitted to the professional stage, they literally took over the entire minstrel convention. Like their white imitators, they used burnt cork and thickened lips in an attempt to imitate their plantation forefathers. At the same time, Negro composers, singers, and especially dancers, gave new life to this form of entertainment, and the minstrel companies prospered.

One of the first all-Negro minstrel troupes was organized by a Negro named Charles Hicks, in 1865. These trained musicians and performers were billed as the Georgia Minstrels, who toured through the South.

Although Hicks was an able director and manager, he encountered financial difficulties, possibly due to the South's lack of enthusiasm for minstrelsy. The troupe was finally taken over by Charles Callender, who later engaged Charles Frohman as advance agent. Jack Haverly later bought the company from Callender, and the group was headed by Billy Kersands, one of the greatest minstrels his day and of all time, and by Sam Lucas.

It was with this group that Bland found himself associated. Many of the members he added to his list of friends. His close attachment and friendship for Billy Kersands were immortalized in the lyrics of "De Golden Wedding," and in later years Bland's never-faltering loyalty to Kersands was proved over and over again. Bland's circle of friends was not confined to towns; he became equally well-known in the larger cities throughout the United States, and counted among his friends, writers, musicians, prize fighters, actors, and even clergymen.

His first season on the road with Haverly's was a prosperous one, so prosperous indeed that the show never even reached New York. Colonel Haverly had sent the troupe out with a good-sized bank roll, and this was added to at every performance. Besides, near the end of the tour, Bland's songs were being sold in the lobby of the theater during intermission and after the show, and the Colonel was getting a percentage of the profits.

At the end of his first season, Bland, too, was reasonably wealthy. The songs he had

had published were paying good royalties and were being sold all over the country, spurred on their way to popularity by the "plugs" received at minstrel show performances.

When the troupe finally disbanded, Bland returned to Washington. He had an innate love for what he called his old home town; he was also anxious to see Mannie Friend, for he had missed her companionship and her loyal help.

Bland's success had driven the wedge between them that Mannie had always feared. There are many authorities who suspect that she had contributed no small part in the writing of some of his lyrics. Although there is not sufficient evidence to prove this, it is fairly safe to assume that when he and she were young she was the inspiration for some of his best compositions.

During one of their many rifts, Mannie wrote a poem entitled "You Could Have Been True," and pleaded with Jimmy to write the music. The words of this song, more than any other, bear out the prediction that Mannie had made years before when she and Jimmy had talked about their future. Just when the final break came with the one person who had inspired him more than any other is not known. But however or whenever it occurred, it is clear that as Jimmy's public acclaim grew, his interest in Mannie waned, until at last his first love, "show business," claimed him heart and soul.

CHAPTER 12

MATINEE IDOL

After the publication of "Carry Me Back to Old Virginny," Bland's compositions were eagerly sought after by music publishers. Upon his return from Europe, some of his song sheets advertised him as "The World's Greatest Minstrel Man." On Capitol Hill in Washington, where he was well-known and had many friends, he was affectionately known to all as the "Melody Man."

Pennsylvania Avenue was his Broadway, and he spent as many of his nights and days on that thoroughfare as possible.

As the Melody Man, he was responsible for some of the songs popular in election campaigns. "The Missouri Hound Dog," with its sad refrain, "You Gotta Stop Kicking My Hound Around," was one of his early compositions, and was used years later in the Champ Clark headquarters at the Democratic Convention in Baltimore.

He wrote a song for another campaign called "Hot Time in Our Town," and later "In the Old Town Tonight." Each of these airs has been used in many election campaigns since that time.

He composed but few marches, but the best known is probably "Dandy Black Brigade," a song and chorus that immortalized the memory of a colored National Guard Regiment marching down Broadway.

Some of Bland's compositions reveal a side of his character that was overshadowed by his lighter compositions. The lyrics of "Father's Growing Old" and "The Old-Fashioned Cottage" bear a tinge of the sentimentalist.

"Listen to the Silver Trumpets" is a number that stirs the blood, after the fashion of the compositions of Sousa, the March King. In this music Bland had the rare gift of producing sounds that imitated bugle calls or the shuffling of shoes on a dance floor.

It is not too much to say that many of the song hits of a decade ago or even some of the current ones owe their inspiration to the Bland influence. The opening bars of the chorus of "There's a Long, Long Trail," the outstanding song hit of First World War, are identical, note for note, to the music of "In the Evening by the Moonlight." Just as Bland was ever quick to acknowledge the influence of Stephen Foster in his compositions, so has the Melody Man himself influenced many of our present-day composers.

Musical detectives have found other instances in which the Bland music is duplicated in present-day musical arrangements. This does not necessarily imply plagiarism, for the copyright laws and the rules of the broadcasting companies, and even the American Society of Composers, Authors and Publishers, permit the lifting of any four bars from one song into another. Even if this practice infringed on the copyright law, nothing could be done about it in the case of the published Bland songs, since they have been in public domain since the turn of the century.

Although the young composer did not follow the advice of the minstrel man, George Primrose, to get his song "Carry Me Back to Old Virginny" copyrighted immediately upon publication in 1874, he did manage to have this done some six years later.

Bland could rightly be called composer, lyricist, jokester, skit writer and banjoist, and yet he had another facet to his character—a bit of inventive ability. Bland, the composer, was likewise Bland, the inventor. Before the turn of the century, he had made an outstanding contribution to the value of the banjo by the addition of a fifth string.

This was not an idea of the moment, but no doubt was a development that evolved from his long association with the instrument. In some quarters it was said that the banjo was his great love, that he thought more of it than he did even of any human being, including Mannie Friend, and perhaps his family.

Of one thing there is certainty: Bland knew the limitations of the banjo, and because of this he knew how it could be improved.

In his day, the banjo, the only truly American musical instrument, was still in its original form and had only four strings.

Of Southern origin, it is believed that the banjo was an outgrowth of the African tom-tom, the drum head combined with the shank of a violin.

Today the old four-string banjos are in great demand by collectors. When the first five-string banjo was introduced, it immediately became known as the Bland banjo and became the rage of the musical world.

By 1881, when the Forty-seventh Congress was in session, the songs of Bland had swept the nation and were sung in Washington constantly.

On March 4, 1881, James A. Garfield was inaugurated President of the United States, and a Negro band came swinging down Pennsylvania Avenue playing some of the Bland melodies, which had been stepped up to march time. Seemingly, all Bland's melodies lend themselves to any tempo imaginable. Some of the lullabies sound just as stirring in march time as they do in waltz tempo. "Carry Me Back to Old Virginny" received its baptism on that Inauguration Day as a march—something it was certainly never intended to be. As the band passed the stands, playing his now famous song, Bland received the plaudits of those about him.

Bland's re-entry into the field of his former conquests was really auspicious. His salary by that time had reached the then princely sum of ten thousand dollars for a single season, the highest ever paid a minstrel man up to that period. Indeed, few legitimate stage stars in those days ever attained such opulence.

Bland joined Haverly's Minstrels and the troupe departed for England, where they were billed as Haverly's European Minstrels. They rehearsed all the way to London, and when they reached the English capital, they became a sensation practically overnight. The British had heard about plantation melodies, for some of the Foster songs had already been heard in England, but audiences at Her Majesty's Theater had seen few Negro minstrel performers.

Bland himself was an immediate hit, and the songs he sang received enthusiastic praise. The critics raved over a brand of entertainment they had never known before. As a result of the London engagement, some of Bland's best-known songs, such as "Carry Me Back to Old Virginny," became popular in the music halls. Unfortunately, the public was not aware that Bland should have been given credit for these works, because his name was not printed on the original English programs as author and composer.

From London, the Bland melodies reached the music halls of Liverpool, Old Chester, and Manchester. From England they crossed the Channel to Ireland, where they were sung in Dublin. No one credited Bland with them, however; everybody hailed them as new Stephen Foster songs.

That fact bothered and worried Bland. Naturally, he wanted credit for his own works; he wanted recognition, but he had to fight hard to get it. He finally achieved it by offering his services for every charity he heard of and by accepting none of the proceeds, not even his own expenses. Wherever he appeared, he was inevitably introduced as the author of his own songs, and as a consequence his fame spread, and he was soon the rage of London.

Bland, a minstrel man, was one of the first American performers to make such an impression on the music-loving capital. Eventually his fame reached the Prince of Wales, Albert Edward, who was later to become King of England.

Albert Edward, the eldest son of Queen Victoria, was a generous patron of music and of charities, and while he was engaged in these activities, he became acquainted with the works of James A. Bland. The minstrel man had given generously of his time and talents, had appeared in many garden festivals at the homes of the wealthy, and at minor affairs. One day the Prince of Wales expressed a desire to hear the American minstrel sing. As a result, Bland received an invitation to give a command performance at Buckingham Palace.

The Royal Family enjoyed Bland's music and songs very much, and the Prince of Wales applauded heartily, for this sort of entertainment was new to him. Bland was obliged to give several encores, which he did with all the charm he possessed.

Although Bland had composed some of his songs while touring the United States with the Haverly Minstrels, several of them were now being heard in London for the first time. Wisely, he had hitherto withheld several of them so that they would not be put on the market.

Colonel Haverly constantly prodded Bland to introduce new songs into the show, but Bland was reticent about giving his entire repertoire. He knew that much of his music had been stolen; he was well aware that a good many of his compositions had been attributed to Stephen Foster, and so he clung to his newer numbers. When he was firmly established in London, however, he had a change of heart and was inspired to give his audiences his best.

Consequently, many of the now famous Bland songs were launched on the other side of the Atlantic, but sometimes they did not reach these shores until many months after their release.

Bland liked London, and London liked Bland. He felt perfectly at home with these people who had taken him to their hearts. The music halls there were so much better and more popular than the imitation of them in Washington, that he was inclined to stay in England. When the time came for

Colonel Jack Haverly to close the London run and bring his minstrels home, Bland decided to remain there. By this time he had plenty of money, and likewise many friends in London.

Until the very last moment, he had told no one of his intention. Had he done so, he would have had plenty of company, for many of the members of the troupe would have stayed with him, partly because they would have enjoyed being with him and partly for the experience.

After all the good-bys had been said and the ship had pulled out, Bland turned back to the gaiety of London. He had rented a little place in Battersea Park, known as the Old Dog's House section, and had also hired an agent, who was able to book him in the better class clubs and restaurants. Here he repeated his Washington performances and triumphs.

Whenever Bland was part of a minstrel show, he appeared in blackface. As an individual performer, he stepped out on the stage without make-up.

It was while he was in London that he began his career as a man of fashion. He loved to dress well, and his wardrobe, made for him by famous tailors, characterized him as the well-dressed gentleman.

In a sense he had become an idol of the British and for his public appearances he was billed as "The Idol of the Music Halls."

From London, his songs traveled across the English Channel, to Paris and Berlin. After another summer in London, Bland followed them and toured the Continent. He wandered through the famous beer gardens of Bremen and Berlin, where he could listen to the music, although the lyrics had been translated into German. After his visits to Bremen and Berlin, he continued on to Coblenz and Cologne, where his ballads were equally as popular as they had been in England and other parts of Germany.

The German people were sympathetic to Bland's music. Hans Wunderlich, an outstanding musician of the day, later solo cornetist with the United States Marine Band, said that "Before the turn of the century, only three American composers made an appreciable dent in the German consciousness: John Philip Sousa, James A. Bland, and Stephen Foster."

The Germans liked the Sousa marches because they were stirring, exciting and militant; they loved the melody and rhythm of the Foster and Bland plantation songs.

In Hamburg, where Bland gave an outdoor concert in a public park, the Germans were fascinated by the banjo, an instrument they had not heard or seen before. Although they were more accustomed to the tones of trombones and bass horns and other brasses of the usual German band, they took an immediate liking to this new stringed instrument. They also enjoyed keenly the songs Bland sang, even though many of his listeners did not understand English. So popular was this master of music that he was offered a return engagement not only in Hamburg, but in all the other places he had visited. Instead, he decided to go back to England and remain there awhile before sailing for America. Bland had made such a niche for himself in London that he could have lived there the rest of his life if he had wanted to.

In the years that followed, it has been revealed that he spent considerable time abroad.

CHAPTER 13

THE CURTAIN CALL

BY THE TIME BLAND WAS THIRTY-SIX years old, he and his songs were known not only throughout this country but also on the Continent of Europe. He was at the peak of his career, the height of his glory.

The first summer in that period now known as the "Gay Nineties" proved to be the busiest one in Bland's life. Now that he was a recognized composer as well as a minstrel man, his services were more than ever in demand. His songs were becoming more popular in the big cities, and publishers were on his trail for more and more of his compositions.

Most of them were top-notch; others, though good, were routine, but each one had a specific appeal.

At this time he was turning out tunes at the rate of one a week, for melodies flowed from him.

In the launching of these songs Bland had many willing helpers—"pluggers" they were called, a term that became popular during this period. One of these song pluggers was Billy Emerson, a fellow minstrel man; George Primrose was another who was ever ready to help out a friend whom he had started on a career away back in the early days in Baltimore. Billy Kersands, the comedian, and a long-time friend of Bland's, never lost a chance to plug one of his songs.

Bland's royalty checks were beginning to show what promotion actually means, for one check for more than five thousand dollars represented a year's sale of his compositions.

Even though he had never married, Bland loved children, and they were attracted to him. When he was in Washington he was always in the center of a group of youngsters, for they liked to hear him strum and play the banjo, and to hear him sing his songs. Usually these were his sisters' and brothers' children and their friends. It was undoubtedly this pleasant association that caused Bland to express his love for children in many of his songs.

Through his relatives' children, and others, Bland helped at many charitable affairs. In those days, before motion pictures, radio and television took over, there were all sorts of church festivals, outdoor garden parties, picnics and excursions. At these parties he was always in demand. He and his young protégés would stage an outdoor show in the summertime when he wasn't on a minstrel tour.

In later years, Gus Edwards, a vaudevillian who did the same sort of entertainment, admitted that he had learned a lesson from Jimmy Bland. "Jimmy Bland first got me interested in kids as musical timber," Gus Edwards once told a friend. It was Edwards who wrote "School Days, Dear Old Golden Rule Days." It was Edwards who had brought out such stars as Eddie Cantor and Georgie Jessel. Walter Winchell also played in Edwards' act on the old Keith Circuit.

Bland had seen Gus Edwards get his start in show business; he had heard many of his songs and even helped him with some of them. It was Bland who gave Edwards a fine piece of advice.

"You make a lot of money in the songwriting business, Gus, if the songs hit. But you spend it all. I'm through. If I had a chance to do it all over again, I'd try to save something."

"How can you?" Gus asked, knowing show business and its temptations.

"An insurance man was telling me about life insurance annuities the other day, but you've got to have some money," Bland said.

"I just made a hundred thousand dollars," Gus bragged.

"Then put it with a good life insurance company."

Gus followed Bland's advice, and as a consequence, he and his wife were able to live in the fashionable Astor Hotel in New York until their respective deaths, all because Jimmy Bland, who had learned the hard way, could tell others how to protect themselves, but who did not provide for any security for himself because of his own extravagance.

"I always bless the memory of Jimmy Bland," Gus Edwards once said to the manager of Keith's Theatre in Washington. "He did for me what he didn't do for himself. I knew him when he was on his last legs and he was a swell guy."

Had Bland been of a different temperament, he might have given the nation more songs, just as he might have lived longer had he not thrown himself into the fervor of high living as it was known in his day. Some of his boyhood friends lived to be more than ninety years of age, and it was from these men and women that many of the stories of his life were gathered—a hectic life that ended all too soon at fifty-seven.

From all accounts, Bland never seemed to have relaxed, no matter where he was or what he was doing, even on vacation. Constantly on the move, seldom resting, filled with boundless activity—all were part of his life.

If events were dull for him in America, he packed his clothes and went to Europe. When he tired of the European scene, he came back home. Wherever he was, he managed to have a good time—that is until the last year of his life. Then fortune turned against him.

When Bland returned to Washington to stay, he knew no one in public office and most of his old friends on Capitol Hill had disappeared. Hardly anyone knew the one-time famous minstrel man. Mannie Friend, his erstwhile sweetheart, had died.

Bland was despondent. In London he had had his last fling. The minstrel shows were no longer a novelty, for minstrel men had given way to vaudevillians. The curtain had descended on Bland and his type of entertainment.

During the last years of his stay in England he had featured such songs as "The Old Homestead," "The Farmer's Daughter," "Father's Growing Old," and "Christmas Dinner." These were his own compositions; today most of these songs are forgotten. It is true that similar titles have since been used for plays and motion pictures—notably "The Old Homestead" and "The Farmer's Daughter." Bland had an ear for titles. He once confessed that titles and lyrics came to him easily, but he sometimes had to struggle

with a tune, although he knew the importance of the melody.

When Bland was in his heyday in England, he had taken London over completely, and as a result had plenty of money, but he left there in the early 1900's absolutely penniless. All he had in the world was his fare back to New York. When he arrived there the few minstrel troupes in existence had gone out on the road, so there was no work in the theater for him. Disconsolate, penniless, forlorn, he journeyed on to Washington.

Bland arrived in the Capital blind baggage. It was a far different homecoming than his earlier ones, when he had been wined and dined and lionized.

Word soon spread around the city that the famous composer was broke. A boyhood friend, William Silence, gave him assistance and provided desk space for him in Silence's downtown law office. Bland was assured that this was his sanctum, the place where he could write and compose whenever the mood struck him. But he was not in the mood. The old flair was gone. Listlessly, he wandered around, looking for old pals and cronies. Few knew him.

Finally, he settled down to work, but this proved to be his last effort. It was a struggle, but he managed to compose the music and write the lyrics for a musical production called "The Sporting Girl."

Irony of ironies, Bland received less money for this entire production than he had previously been paid for his least-known song. He sold the entire output, words and music, for two hundred fifty dollars.

"The Sporting Girl" followed the typical musical comedy design of the day. It was made up of two acts and contained eighteen songs. Strange as it may seem, the original book had been outlined years before by Mannie Friend. Mannie and Bland had intended to collaborate on it, but somehow they never accomplished their ambition.

Bland had now to face reality. During his long absence in Europe, Mannie had collected some of the old love lyrics they had set aside for future use. Their separation and Bland's indifference had broken her heart, but bravely she had saved the poems he had written to her when they were classmates. These she had cherished, and when she realized that she would not live to see Jimmy again, she turned them over to a member of his family. Some of these poems were the basis for several love songs in "The Sporting Girl."

With the small return on this venture, the man who had once enjoyed the highest earnings in his field, now lost heart.

One day, without saying a word to anyone, not even bidding his few remaining friends good-by, Bland packed what meager belongings he possessed and went back to Philadelphia, the scene of his early childhood.

At that time the minstrels were still popular in that city. Bland tried to join a troupe playing on Market Street, but he was unsuccessful. It was the same old story. They did not want him, although they did use his songs.

Although he was still able to laugh at the quirks of fate, he knew he had reached the end of the road. His heart was heavy; his spirit weary.

Everything seemed to have turned against the gay minstrel of the Gay Nineties. His lodgings were dismal. Even the weather mocked him. It was the end of March, he was in poor health, and as a result caught a terrific cold. In less than five weeks he took his final curtain call.

Penniless, alone, without friends, James A. Bland died on May 6, 1911.

No death notice for the once famous minstrel appeared in any newspaper. No feature story told who he was or what he had done. No tribute was paid to the composer of the now famous "Carry Me Back to Old Virginny," by this time on the lips of young and old alike. The man who had used "the song in his heart" to entertain two continents died unwept, unhonored, and forgotten.

CARRY ME BACK TO OLD VIRGINNY

Moderato

1. Car-ry me back to old Vir-gin-ny, There's where the cot-ton and the
2. Car-ry me back to old Vir-gin-ny, There let me live 'till I

corn and ta-toes grow,   There's where the birds war-ble sweet in the spring-time,
with-er and de-cay,   Long by the old Dis-mal Swamp have I wan-der'd,

There's where the old dark-ey's heart am long'd to go.   There's where I la-bor'd so
There's where the old dark-ey's life will pass a-way.   Mas - sa and mis-sis have

hard for old mas-sa,   Day af - ter day in the field of yel - low corn,
long gone be-fore me,   Soon we will meet on that bright and gold - en shore,

No place on earth do I love more sin-cere-ly
There we'll be hap - py and free from all sor - row,

Than old Vir - gin - ny, the state where I was born.
There's where we'll meet and we'll nev - er part no more.

rit.

CHORUS
SOPRANO

Car - ry me back to old Vir-gin-ny, There's where the cot - ton and the

ALTO

TENOR

Car - ry me back to old Vir-gin-ny, There's where the cot - ton and the

BASS

corn and ta-toes grow, There's where the birds war - ble

corn and ta-toes grow, There's where the birds war - ble

sweet in the spring-time, There's where this old dark-ey's heart am long'd to go.

sweet in the spring-time, There's where this old dark-ey's heart am long'd to go.

rit. **Repeat pp last time**

rit.

rit.

YOU COULD HAVE BEEN TRUE

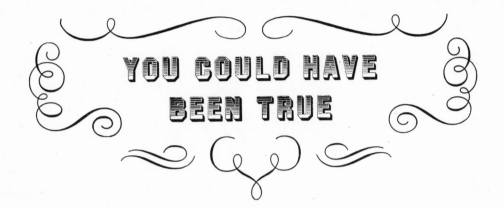

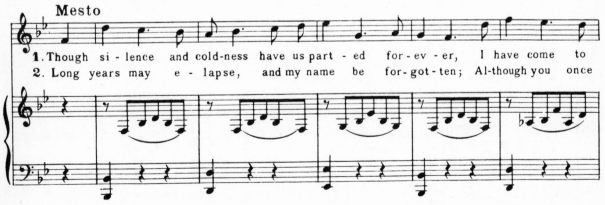

tell, with   deep pain in   my heart,   For the sake of   the past and the
fear'd   was   my love for   you true,   But my love you   ac - cept - ed, first

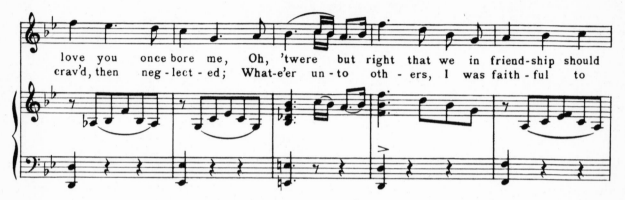

love you   once bore   me,   Oh, 'twere   but right that we   in friend-ship should
crav'd, then   neg - lect - ed;   What-e'er   un - to   oth - ers,   I was faith - ful   to

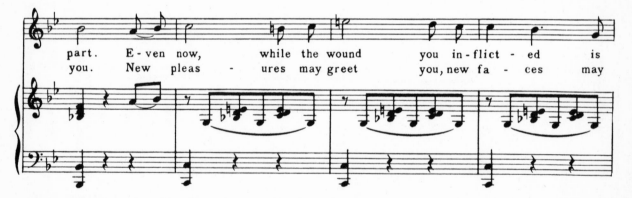

part.   E - ven now,   while the wound   you in-flict - ed   is
you.   New pleas -   ures may greet   you, new fa - ces   may

ach - ing,   A   voice   in my heart pleads in   soft   tones   for you;   Who
meet   you, New   loves for a   time   your   heart may en - twine;   Their

wav - er'd   and fal - ter'd,   were fic - kle   and al - ter'd;   Oh,
friend - ship,   though new - er,   can nev - er   be tru - er,   Or

why   were you false,   when you could have been   true?
ev -   er as ten - der, or faith - ful   as   mine.

CHORUS
SOPRANO
Why were you false,   why so un - kind, How could you for - get one who

ALTO

TENOR

Why were you false,   why so un - kind, How could you for - get one who

BASS

lived but for you? The vows that were spo - ken, by

lived but for you?

you have been bro - ken; Fare-well for - ev - er__ why were you un - true?

Fare-well for - ev - er__ why were you un - true?

IN THE EVENING BY THE MOONLIGHT

Con dolce maniera

1. In de ebe-ning by de moon-light when dis dar-ky's work was o - ver, We would
2. In de ebe-ning by de moon-light when de watch-dog would be sleep-ing, In de

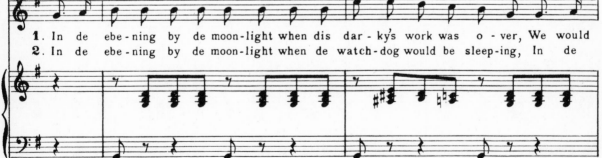

gath - er round de fire, 'till de hoe - cake it was done. Den we
cor - ner near de fire - place, be - side de ole arm - chair, Whar Aunt

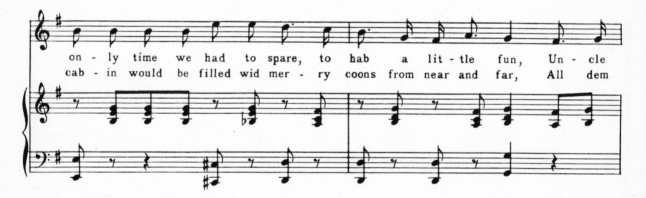

all would eat our sup - per, af - ter dat we'd clear de kitch - en, Dat's de
Chlo - e used to sit and tell de Pic - ca - nin - nies sto - ries, And de

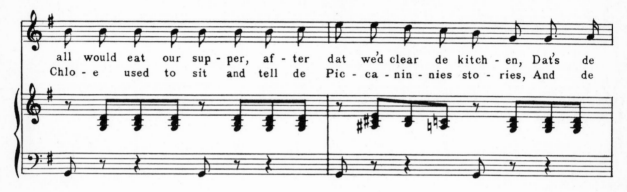

on - ly time we had to spare, to hab a lit - tle fun, Un - cle
cab - in would be filled wid mer - ry coons from near and far, All dem

Gabe would take de fid - dle down, dat hung up - on de wall, While de
hap - py times we used to hab, will ne'er re - turn a - gain, Eb - 'ry -

sil - v'ry moon was shin - ing clear and bright, How de old folks would en - joy it, they would

thing was den so mer-ry gay and bright, And I neb - er will for-get it, when our

sit all night and lis - ten, As we sang in de ebe-ning by de moon - light.

dai - ly toil was o - ber, How we sang in de ebe-ning by de moon - light.

CHORUS
SOPRANO

In de ebe-ning by de moon-light, you could hear us dar-kies sing - ing, In de

ALTO

TENOR

In de ebe-ning by de moon-light, you could hear us dar-kies sing - ing, In de

BASS

ebe-ning by de moon-light you could hear de ban-jo ring-ing, How de old folks would en-joy it,

ebe-ning by de moon-light you could hear de ban-jo ring-ing, How de old folks would en-joy it,

They would sit all night and lis-ten, As we sang in de ebe-ning by de moon-light.

They would sit all night and lis-ten, As we sang in de ebe-ning by de moon-light.

DANCING ON DE KITCHEN FLOOR

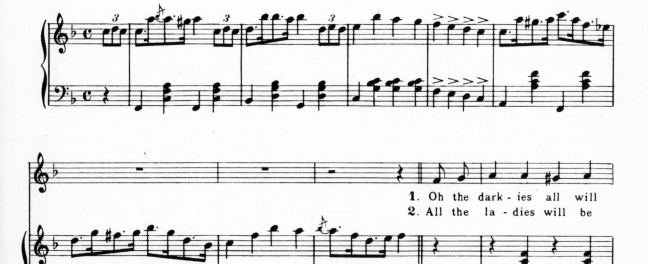

1. Oh the dark - ies all will
2. All the la - dies will be

have a ju - bi - lee, Such a gath-er - ing there nev - er was be - fore, Oh how
dressed so ver - y neat, Ev -'ry - bod - y will look ver - y nice and clean, When we

hap - py ev -'ry one will be, As we dance up - on the kitch - en floor.
dar - kies prom - en - ade the street, Ev -'ry - thing will be just like a dream.

There'll be walk - ing for the cake, all the
There is dan - dy Dick and Pete, they will

la - dies' hearts well break, When we all com - mence to do the prom - e - nade, Bet - sey
ex - er - cise their feet, And the yal - ler gals will do the same, you see, We will

 [84]

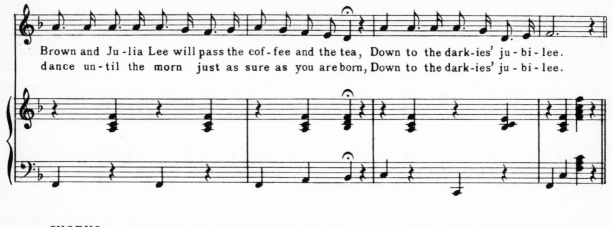

Brown and Ju-lia Lee will pass the cof-fee and the tea, Down to the dark-ies' ju-bi-lee.
dance un-til the morn just as sure as you are born, Down to the dark-ies' ju-bi-lee.

CHORUS

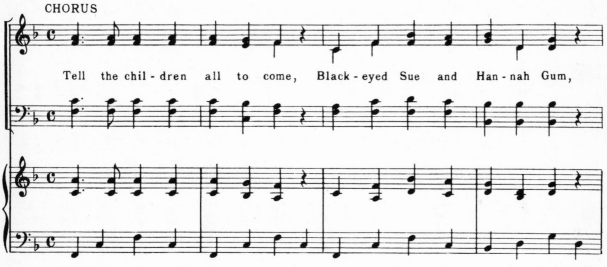

Tell the chil-dren all to come, Black-eyed Sue and Han-nah Gum,

Mu-sic ring-ing, dar-kies sing-ing, Ev-'ry one a-gree,

Grease the floor and close the win-dow, Don't for-get to tell Ma-lin-da

That we all are get-ting read-y for the ju - bi -lee.

DANCE

BREAK

GABRIEL'S BAND

1. Ga-briel's gwine to blow his trum-pet, And he'll blow it in de morn-ing, So you'd
2. Send a tel - e - gram to Di - nah, If it ain't too hard to find her, Tell her
3. When de bells com-mence a ring-ing, When you hear the chil-dren sing-ing, Dat's de

bet - ter eb - 'ry - one be wide a -wake; Tell de chil-dren one and all, When dey
that the gos-pel ship am gwine to sail; She will cook de glo - ry soup, And you'll
time dat we will mas-ti-cate de ham; Eb - 'ry one will hab a seat, Den we'll

hear de trum-pet call, To get read - y for to eat de gos-pel cake; Tell Ma -
nev - er catch de croup, And she's gwine to eat up cot-ton by de bale; So put
all com-mence to eat, And we'll par - a - lize de tur-key and de lamb; Den you'd

til - da, Jake, and Han-nah, For to speak to Doc - tor Tan-ner, And to
on your gold - en slip-pers, Bring a - long your wa - ter dip-pers, Den you
bathe your feet in hon - ey, It will make you feel so fun - ny; Put some

tell him dat he can't fast an - y - more: Dar'll be lots of chick-en-pie, He can
get up bright and ear - ly in de morn: Hab your tick-ets in your hand, When you
grease up - on your al - a - bas-ter brow: Make your will out in the fall, When you

eat it on de sly When old Ga - bry ain't a peep-ing through de door.
jine old Ga-briel's band, Kase we'se go - ing up to glo - ry sure's you're born.
hear de trum-pet call, For old Ga-briel am a-wait-ing on you now.

CHORUS

Join old Ga-briel's Band, and trav-el through dis hap-py land, We'll

Join old Ga-briel's Band, and trav-el through dis hap-py land, We'll

all wear dia-monds on our hands, And eat the gos-pel chow-der.

all wear dia-monds on our hands, And eat the gos-pel chow-der.

Interlude

OH! LUCINDA

1. I know a charm-ing lit-tle girl, Her name it is Lu-cin-da. And
2. Next day while walk-ing down the street, I chance to meet this fai-ry. And
3. She is a love-ly crea-ture, And the boys on her are cra-zy. And

ev-'ry time I pass the house, She's peep-ing through the win-dow. She's
as she slow-ly tripped a-long, Her step was light and air-y. I
all through-out the neigh-bor-hood, They say that she's a dai-sy. Her

got such love-ly jet black eyes, And long black cur-ly hair. And
fol-lowed her a block or more, And tried to catch her eye. But
fea-tures are so per-fect, And her form is so com-plete. The

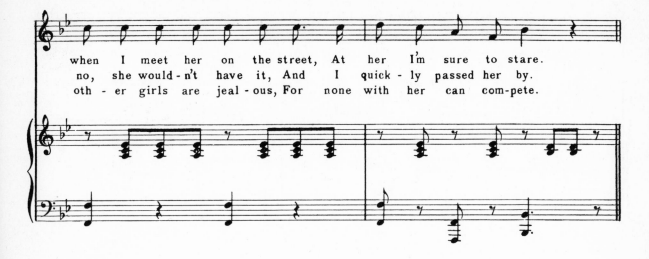

when I meet her on the street, At her I'm sure to stare.
no, she would-n't have it, And I quick-ly passed her by.
oth-er girls are jeal-ous, For none with her can com-pete.

CHORUS

Oh! Lu-cin-da you're the sweet-est girl I know,

Oh! Lu-cin-da I would like to be your beau. You're a

dar - ling, you're a dai - sy, You're a fai - ry, you're a dove. I'd

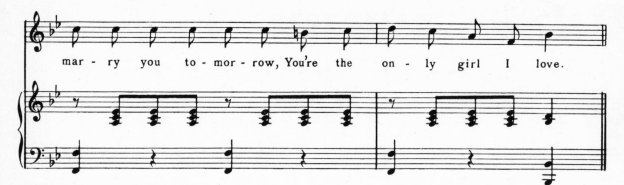

mar - ry you to - mor - row, You're the on - ly girl I love.

DANCE

BREAK

OH, DEM GOLDEN SLIPPERS!

VOICE

1. Oh, my gold-en slip-pers am laid a-way, Kase I don't 'spect to wear 'em till my
2. Oh, my ole ban-jo hangs on de wall, Kase it ain't been tuned since
3. So, it's good-bye, chil-dren, I will have to go Whar de rain don't fall or de

wed-din' day, And my long-tail'd coat, dat I loved so well, I will
way last fall, But de darks all say we will hab a good time, When we
wind don't blow, And yer ul-ster coats, why, yer will not need, When yer

wear up in de char-iot in de morn; And my long white robe dat I
ride up in de char-iot in de morn; Dar's ole Brud-der Ben and
ride up in de char-iot in de morn; But yer gold-en slip-pers must be

bought last June, I'm gwine to git changed Kase it fits too soon, And de
Sis - ter Luce, Dey will tel - e-graph de news to Un-cle Bac-co Juice, What a
nice and clean, And yer age must be Just sweet six-teen, And yer

ole grey hoss dat I used to drive, I will hitch him to de char-iot in de morn.
great camp-meet-in' der will be dat day, When we ride up in de char-iot in de morn.
white kid gloves yer will have to wear, When yer ride up in de char-iot in de morn.

CHORUS

SOPRANO *(First time pp, repeat ff)*

Oh, dem gold-en slip-pers! Oh, dem gold-en slip-pers! Gold-en slip-pers I'm

ALTO

TENOR

Oh, dem gold-en slip-pers! Oh, dem gold-en slip-pers! Gold-en slip-pers I'm

BASS

(First time pp, repeat ff)

gwine to wear, be-case dey look so neat ;   Oh, dem gold-en slip-pers! Oh, dem

gwine to wear, be-case dey look so neat ;   Oh, dem gold-en slip-pers! Oh, dem

gold-en slip-pers! Gold-en slip-pers Ise gwine to wear, To walk de gold-en   street.   street.

gold-en slip-pers! Gold-en slip-pers Ise gwine to wear, To walk de gold-en   street.   street.

THE OLD FASHIONED COTTAGE

1. The old fash-ion'd cot - tage, the place I lov'd so well, The spot where my Moth - er and
2. I long to re-turn to the cot-tage once a - gain, To think of it, fills me with

Fa - ther used to dwell, Oh, how oft - en I've stroll'd thro' the fields of grow-ing corn, Near the
sor - row and with pain, Man - y years now have pass'd since I left my dear old home, To

old fash-ion'd cot - tage, The place I was born, I re-mem - ber the gar - den, the
wan - der a-broad thro' this wide world to roam, The spot has grown lone - ly, that

grove and the mill, And the lit - tle frame school house, that stood by the hill, But with
once was so bright, Where oft Moth - er kiss'd her dear chil - dren good-night, Oh, how

all   its   sur - round - ings,   I   loved   none   so   well,   As   the
mer - ry   the   birds   sang,   their   sweet   songs   of   yore   As   they

old   fash - ion'd   cot - tage,   Where   I   once   used   to   dwell.
perch'd   on   the   ma - ple,   Near   the   old   cot - tage   door

CHORUS

SOPRANO

The   old   fash - ion'd   cot - tage,   the   place   I   was   born,   My

ALTO

TENOR

The   old   fash - ion'd   cot - tage,   the   place   I   was   born,

BASS

home once so hap-py, has grown so for-lorn, How I long to re-turn to the

home I love so well, The old fash-ion'd cot-tage where I once used to dwell.

The old fash-ion'd cot-tage where I once used to dwell.